A Sentry Guide to

**Somerset Maugham's
The Razor's Edge**

ISBN Paperback 978-1-989647-19-6

A Byrd Press Publication
Toronto
www.byrdpress.com
publisher@byrdpress.com

cover design R.H. Mason
All images in this Book were generated with the assistance of AI in 2023.

A Sentry Guide to

**Somerset Maugham's
The Razor's Edge**

RISHIKESH 1930s

Rishikesh has been a significant spiritual and yoga center in India for many decades, and it was particularly popular among Western seekers and spiritual tourists in the 1930s. During that time, Rishikesh was known for its serene and picturesque location on the banks of the Ganges River in the foothills of the Himalayas, making it an attractive destination for those seeking spiritual growth and enlightenment.

Welcome to "The Razor's Edge"

"The Razor's Edge" is a thought-provoking novel that explores themes of self-discovery, spirituality, and the search for meaning in the aftermath of World War I.

Set in the post-war era, the story follows the journeys of several characters, but at its heart is Larry Darrell, a World War I veteran who embarks on a quest for self-realization and enlightenment in the wake of the disillusionment caused by the War and societal changes.

As Larry seeks deeper meaning in life beyond the pursuit of material success, he travels to Europe and later to South-East Asia, immersing himself in Eastern spirituality and mysticism.

Along the way, he encounters various characters who represent different paths in life, including his fiancée, Isabel, who is driven by conventional societal values.

Maugham himself is a character in the novel, serving as the narrator and observer of the characters' lives. His presence allows for insightful commentary on their choices and actions.

"The Razor's Edge" is a profound exploration of the human condition, the impact of war, and the quest for authenticity and purpose in a world marked by social change and disillusionment. It raises questions about the nature of happiness, the pursuit of one's true self, and the conflicts between societal expectations and individual aspirations.

Table of Contents

How to Use this Book

This book is meant to be used by educators, auto-didacts, students, book and reading groups and lifelong learners.

The primary organization of this book is that of a graduate school level syllabus. Provided is:

- A critical examination of the Book being studied, that is most likely a bit more idiosyncratic than the standard "notes" options that help a reader, or non-reader, pass a test of some sort.
- A "typical" Graduate-Level Course outline
- A Reading list, or Lists
- A breakdown of each topic covered, by week
- Follow up questions for the group or for personal reflection
- Ancillary topics for discussion, personal reflection or further study

The organization of this book as a graduate-level course, is functional and arbitrary. The format was chosen because it is easier to go from formal and comprehensive to causal and tangential, than visa versa.

The formal-first approach allows several topics to be explored in depth. It is suited for a reference to be used in an educational institute or structured learning environment. It is also suited for a hunt-and-peck, grazing approach, that might be best suited for the individual or group seeking a few insights or not-so-obvious pathways into the text to bring to their own reflections or discussions.

With this in mind, the format can be used any number of ways. Suggested modifications to this format for reading groups wishing to compress the discussion into one or two meetings will find options for doing so in the final section of this book.

This book presents a collection of ideas and starting points for conversation about the human condition and universal human themes. It can be read as a Post-Post-Modern deconstructed non-fiction book, or a catalog of ideas.

It is infinitely customizable.

THE SYLLABUS

This Study Guide is presented as a graduate level course entitled:

Self-Actualization vs. Self-Delusion in American Life: A Study of Somerset Maugham's The Razor's Edge

Course Description:

This graduate-level course explores the theme of self-actualization versus self-delusion in American life through a close examination of Somerset Maugham's classic novel, The Razor's Edge. We will delve into the multifaceted characters and their quests for personal fulfillment, shedding light on the cultural and societal forces that shape their journeys. Through a combination of literary analysis, historical context, and contemporary applications, students will gain a deep understanding of the American pursuit of happiness and self-realization.

Course Objectives:

By the end of the course, students will be able to:

1. Analyze the theme of self-actualization vs. self-delusion in The Razor's Edge and its relevance to American culture.

2. Examine the historical and cultural context of the novel, including the aftermath of World War I and the Jazz Age.

3. Critically assess the characters' motivations, choices, and transformations in the pursuit of self-realization.

4. Explore the ethical and philosophical implications of self-discovery and self-deception.

5. Reflect on the enduring relevance of the novel's themes in contemporary American society.

The course will consist of weekly seminars, lectures, group discussions, and student presentations. Assignments will include critical essays, class participation, and a final research paper on a related topic.

It is understood that a final project will not apply to every Reader of this Book. The final project might be occasional reflection on the text, or a return to the suggested Reading Lists.

Syllabus:

Week 1: Introduction to Self-Actualization vs. Self-Delusion
- Course overview
- The American Dream and its manifestations
- The concept of self-actualization and self-delusion

Week 2: Somerset Maugham and The Razor's Edge
- Somerset Maugham's life and works
- Historical context: Post-World War I America
- Overview of The Razor's Edge. The Characters in Brief.
- Overview of the Novel. The Novel.

Week 3: The Protagonists in Depth
- Characters in Conflict
- Larry Darrell: The quest for truth and self-fulfillment
- Isabel Bradley: Ambition and societal expectations
- Elliott Templeton: The pursuit of social status
- Sophie MacDonald: Coping with trauma and addiction

Week 4: Themes of Self-Actualization
- The Eastern spiritual journey
- Larry's experiences in India and the search for meaning
- Comparing Larry's path with Eastern philosophies

Week 5: Themes of Self-Delusion
- Materialism and societal pressures
- The disillusionment of Isabel and Elliott
- Sophie's struggle with addiction

Week 6: Love and Relationships
- Larry and Isabel: Love and loss
- Sophie and Larry: Compassion and codependency
- The role of relationships in self-discovery
- Personal Relationships in America between WW1 and The Great Depression

Week 7: Ethics and Self-Deception
- Larry's ethical dilemmas
- The consequences of deception in the novel
- Philosophical perspectives on truth and honesty
- Nothing Like the Truh: Power and Deception

Week 8: Contemporary Perspectives
- Modern interpretations of self-actualization
- Back-to-the-Land
- New Traditionalism
- Larry's Individual Way

Week 9: Comparative Analysis
- The Razor's Edge in comparison to other American literature
- Cross-cultural perspectives on self-realization
- Group Encounters: Modern Interpretations of Self-Actualization in the U.S.
- Dangers of Racing After Self-Actualization

Week 10: Student Presentations

Week 11: Discussion and Debate
- Open forum for discussing the novel's themes and contemporary relevance

Week 12: Final Research Papers

Week 13: Course Conclusion
- Reflection on key takeaways and lessons learned
- Wrap-up and evaluation of the course

For Reading Groups and self-guiding lifelong learners, there is no reason to follow the exact flow of the weekly topics, save for weeks 10 and 12, which can be abandoned completely. When taking notes, however, the weekly structure does provide an aid when seeking to return to a particular topic.

The reading list includes supplementary texts to enrich the understanding of the course's themes and to provide additional perspectives on self-actualization, self-delusion, and American life. Students will also have access to digital resources and databases for research purposes. Here are six books that are valuable for this course about "The Razor's Edge".

The Core Reading List:

1. Somerset Maugham - "The Razor's Edge"
- This is the Core text.

2. Maslow, A. H. - "Motivation and Personality"
- Reading both the novel and Maslow's theories can enhance the understanding of the characters' actions and transformations in the story.

-

3. Frankl, Viktor E. - "Man's Search for Meaning"
- Frankl's work explores how people find purpose and strength in difficult times, similar to the characters in the novel.

4. Thoreau, Henry David - "Walden"
- Both works explore themes of self-discovery, simplicity, and the search for meaning in life.

5. Fitzgerald, F. Scott - "The Great Gatsby"
- Both novels delve into the concept of the American Dream and the pursuit of success, happiness, and fulfillment. "The Great Gatsby" examines the hollowness of the American Dream during the Roaring Twenties, while "The Razor's Edge" explores the quest for a meaningful life beyond materialism.

6. Ernest Hemingway - "A Farewell to Arms"
- A classic novel set during World War I, following the story of American ambulance driver Frederic Henry in the Italian army, offering a profound exploration of love, disillusionment, and the harsh realities of war.

Ancillary Reading List 1- U.S. After WW1:

These books collectively provide a rich understanding of the cultural, social, and historical backdrop of the United States and Europe after World War I, making them valuable resources for a course focused on "The Razor's Edge".

1. "The Age of Extremes: A History of the World, 1914-1991" by Eric Hobsbawm
- This comprehensive work provides insights into the social, political, and cultural changes that occurred in the aftermath of World War I.

2. "The Jazz Age: Essays" by F. Scott Fitzgerald
- A collection of essays and writings by F. Scott Fitzgerald, a prominent figure of the Jazz Age, which offers a glimpse into the cultural trends and values of the era.

3. "Paris 1919: Six Months That Changed the World" by Margaret MacMillan
- Focusing on the aftermath of World War I, this book explores the cultural and political dynamics of the post-war world and their influence on society.
-

4. "Weimar Germany: Promise and Tragedy" by Eric D. Weitz
- A comprehensive examination of the Weimar Republic in Germany, a period characterized by political and cultural innovation, but also instability.
-

5. "Modernism: A Very Short Introduction" by Christopher Butler
- This concise introduction to modernism discusses its impact on literature, art, and culture during the early 20th century.

6. "American Nations: A History of the Eleven Rival Regional Cultures of North America" by Colin Woodard
- An exploration of the diverse regional cultures within the United States, shedding light on the cultural tensions and identities that influenced the post-World War I era.

7. "The Harlem Renaissance: Hub of African-American Culture, 1920-1930" by Steven Watson
- Focusing on the cultural explosion in Harlem during the 1920s, this book examines the artistic and intellectual contributions of African Americans.

8. "The Forgotten Man: A New History of the Great Depression" by Amity Shales
- The book provides a historical account and analysis of the Great Depression in the United States. It explores the economic, political, and social aspects of the era, shedding light on the experiences of ordinary Americans who were deeply affected by the economic downturn.

9. "Hard Times: An Oral History of the Great Depression" by Studs Terkel
- "Hard Times" provides a firsthand account of the economic hardships, social changes, and personal struggles that people faced during the Great Depression. The book offers a diverse and authentic perspective on how the Depression affected different segments of society.

10. "The Age of Innocence" by Edith Wharton
- Another novel, The Age of Innocence by Edith Wharton explores the rigid social conventions of the upper class in post-World War I America, offering cultural insights into the period.

And, before you ask, "The Grapes of Wrath" by John Steinbeck is way too important and overwhelming text to put in as "ancillary".

The Characters in "The Razor's Edge" were certainly effected by both WW1 and The Great Depression. Here are two books that delve into the causes of the Great Depression:

1. "The Great Crash 1929" by John Kenneth Galbraith
- In this classic book, economist John Kenneth Galbraith provides a detailed analysis of the events leading up to the Great Depression and the crash of 1929. He explores the economic and social factors that

contributed to the stock market collapse and
the subsequent economic downturn. Galbraith's writing
is both informative and engaging, making it a great
choice for readers interested in understanding the financial
and psychological aspects of the Great Depression.

2. "The Great Depression: A Diary" by Benjamin Roth, edited by James Ledbetter and Daniel B. Roth

- This book offers a unique perspective on the Great
  Depression through the diary entries of Benjamin
  Roth, a lawyer and investor who lived through the era.
  Roth's diary provides firsthand accounts of the financial
  struggles, social changes, and political events of
  the time. The editors provide context and analysis to help
  readers understand the broader causes and consequences
  of the Great Depression.

Reading these two books together will give you a comprehensive
understanding of the causes and impact of the Great Depression
from both a macroeconomic and personal perspective.

And, since we already mentioned "Paris 1919: Six Months That
Changed the World" by Margaret MacMillan, let's add one more title
for context on WW1.

3. "The Great Depression: A Diary" by Benjamin Roth, edited by James Ledbetter and Daniel B. Roth

- This book examines the impact of World War I on the
  global financial system and the profound changes
  it brought about. It delves into the economic consequences
  of the war, the reordering of international politics, and
  how it set the stage for the Great Depression. Adam Tooze
  provides a comprehensive and insightful analysis
  of the war's financial and geopolitical legacies.

The Depressiona nd WW1 title may run a bit far afield for some
discussions, student tastes or educator's intentions, but they are
useful side-trips nevertheless. To return the the core of "The Razor's
Edge", however, let's try something else. A return to the personal
voyage.

Ancillary Reading List 2- Self-Education of a Mystic:

Larry Darrell's journey of self-education as a mystic in "The Razor's Edge" is a, if not "the", central theme of the novel. To help Readers understand this aspect of the character and his transformation, here's a reading list of ten books that delve into mysticism, spirituality, and self-discovery:

1. "The Varieties of Religious Experience" by William James
·   This classic work by William James explores the diversity of religious and mystical experiences, providing a foundational understanding of mysticism.

2. "The Sacred and the Profane: The Nature of Religion" by Mircea Eliade
·   This work, by influential Romanian historian of religion, philosopher, and author, provides a philosophical foundation for characters' spiritual journeys, offering comparative insights into diverse belief systems, and fostering interdisciplinary understanding of the universal concepts of the sacred and the profane in human experience.

3. "The Bhagavad Gita" translated by Eknath Easwaran
·   A revered Hindu scripture, the Bhagavad Gita contains teachings on self-realization and spirituality, which Larry Darrell might have encountered during his quest.

4. "The Tao Te Ching" by Lao Tzu
·   A foundational text in Taoism, the Tao Te Ching explores the concept of the Tao (the Way) and its relevance to self-awareness and inner peace. Note: The "Zhuangzi" offers more humour.

5. "Siddhartha" by Hermann Hesse
·   This novel follows Siddhartha's spiritual journey in search of enlightenment, touching on themes of self-discovery, mysticism, and personal transformation. Though, there is a case to be made that Hesse's "Narcissus and Goldmund" might be just as appropriate, as it revolves around the contrast between intellectual contemplation (Narcissus) and artistic passion (Goldmund).

6. "The Wisdom of Insecurity" by Alan Watts

- Watts discusses the human desire for security and certainty and suggests that embracing uncertainty is a path to greater spiritual understanding.

7. "Autobiography of a Yogi" by Paramahansa Yogananda

- Yogananda's autobiography recounts his spiritual journey in pursuit of self-realization and offers insights into the world of yoga and meditation.

8. "The Power of Now" by Eckhart Tolle

- Tolle explores the concept of living in the present moment and achieving spiritual awakening, a theme that aligns with Larry Darrell's quest.

9. "The Practice of the Wild" by Gary Synder

- In this book, Snyder reflects on the importance of wilderness, ecological awareness, and the pursuit of a more balanced and mindful existence. These themes can resonate with discussions of the characters' search for meaning and self-discovery in "The Razor's Edge."

10. "Mysticism: A Study in the Nature and Development of Spiritual Consciousness" by Evelyn Underhill

- A comprehensive exploration of mysticism, this book provides insights into the mystic's journey and the stages of spiritual development.

These books offer a diverse range of perspectives on mysticism, spirituality, and the pursuit of self-knowledge, providing students with valuable context to understand Larry Darrell's self-education as a mystic in "The Razor's Edge".

And,
One additional book on a practical form of mysticism

"I and Thou" by Martin Buber.
Both works explore profound themes related to spirituality and the human quest for meaning and connection. Here's why I think "I and Thou" complements "The Razor's Edge".

1. Interpersonal Relationships:
"I and Thou" delves into the nature of interpersonal relationships and the concept of encountering the "other" as a Thou, emphasizing genuine, meaningful human connections. This complements the theme of personal relationships and connections explored in "The Razor's Edge."

2. Spiritual Philosophy:
Buber's work presents a philosophy that transcends religious boundaries and explores the spiritual aspects of human existence. It encourages readers to reflect on their relationships with others and with the divine, resonating with the spiritual journeys depicted in "The Razor's Edge."

3. Existential Exploration:
Both "I and Thou" and "The Razor's Edge" touch upon existential questions and the search for authenticity and purpose in life. Buber's exploration of the human encounter with the divine can provide valuable insights into the spiritual quests of characters like Larry Darrell.

4. Ethical Implications:
Buber's work also raises ethical considerations in the context of human relationships and encounters. These ethical dimensions are relevant to the moral dilemmas and choices faced by characters in "The Razor's Edge."

5. Philosophical Depth:
"I and Thou" is a classic work of existential philosophy that encourages deep reflection on the nature of human existence. Its philosophical depth can enhance students' understanding of the spiritual and philosophical dimensions of "The Razor's Edge."

Incorporating Martin Buber's "I and Thou" into the reading list provides students with a valuable philosophical and spiritual framework for understanding the characters' quests for meaning, connection, and authenticity in "The Razor's Edge." It encourages reflection on the nature of human relationships and the search for transcendent experiences, making it a relevant and thought-provoking addition to the course.

Ancillary Reading 3 - The Moon and Sixpence

On the topic of ancillary reading, "The Razor's Edge" and "The Moon and Sixpence", both written by W. Somerset Maugham, explore themes of self-fulfillment, anti-conformity, and the dangers of losing emotional balance.

However, they approach these themes in distinct ways, reflecting differences in character dynamics, settings, and narrative styles:

1. Self-Fulfillment:
"The Razor's Edge": In this novel, the character of Larry Darrell represents a quest for self-fulfillment through spiritual enlightenment and self-realization. Larry's journey takes him to various parts of the world, including India, as he seeks answers to life's profound questions.

"The Moon and Sixpence": In contrast, The Moon and Sixpence explores the life of Charles Strickland, a middle-aged stockbroker who abandons his conventional life to pursue a passion for painting. Strickland's pursuit of self-fulfillment is driven by his desire for artistic expression, even at the expense of societal norms and personal relationships.

2. Anti-Conformity:
"The Razor's Edge": The novel portrays anti-conformity through Larry Darrell's rejection of conventional societal expectations. Larry's decision to eschew materialism and embrace a spiritual path sets him apart from the conformist values of post-World War I America.

"The Moon and Sixpence": In The Moon and Sixpence, Charles Strickland's anti-conformity is centered around his disregard for societal norms, including the abandonment of his family and responsibilities in pursuit of his artistic passion. Strickland's actions defy the conventions of early 20th-century London society.

3. Dangers of Losing Emotional Balance:
 "The Razor's Edge": The novel highlights the importance of emotional balance in the characters' lives. Sophie's tragic descent into alcoholism and despair serves as a cautionary tale about the

dangers of losing emotional equilibrium. Larry Darrell's pursuit of enlightenment, while noble, also leads to emotional challenges and personal sacrifices.

The Moon and Sixpence: Charles Strickland's single-minded pursuit of his art results in emotional detachment and alienation from those around him. His obsession with his craft illustrates the potential consequences of losing emotional balance in the pursuit of one's desires.

While both novels by Somerset Maugham touch on themes of self-fulfillment, anti-conformity, and the dangers of losing emotional balance, they do so in unique ways.

"The Razor's Edge" emphasizes spiritual and philosophical quests for self-fulfillment against the backdrop of post-war America, while "The Moon and Sixpence" focuses on the pursuit of artistic passion and the consequences of anti-conformity in early 20th-century London.

These differences reflect the diverse narrative approaches and character motivations in Maugham's exploration of these themes, yet they still both examine a spectrum of an individual going against the societal norms

They also deal with the motivations, conflicts, causes and effects of "dropping out" of society.

§

Dropping Out

.

The intellectual idea of "dropping out of society" in the Western context has deep historical roots, evolving through various movements and thinkers from ancient times to the 1930s. While there isn't a single origin for this concept, several key developments and philosophers contributed to its formation during this timeframe.

1. Ancient Philosophical Movements (Antiquity):
In ancient Greece, philosophers like Diogenes of Sinope embraced a form of "dropping out" by living in a state of minimalism and self-sufficiency. Diogenes famously advocated for a life in harmony with nature and independent of societal norms.

2. Christian Monasticism (Late Antiquity and Middle Ages):
Christian monasticism, exemplified by figures like St. Anthony of Egypt and St. Benedict, encouraged individuals to withdraw from the secular world and seek spiritual enlightenment in isolated settings, such as deserts or monastic communities.

These movements and philosophies, spanning from ancient times to the 1930s, contributed to the development of the concept of "dropping out of society" during this historical period. They all represented variations of a recurring theme: a desire for autonomy, spiritual growth, and a rejection of the conventions and materialism of their respective societies.

Hobo Culture in the U.S.

Hobo lifestyle began to emerge in the late 19th century and reached its peak during the Great Depression in the 1930s. It persisted into the early 20th century but gradually declined in the decades following World War II. Here is a brief timeline of Hobo Culture in the U.S.

1. Late 19th Century: The late 19th century saw the rise of industrialization and westward expansion in the United States. With the construction of railroads and the demand for manual labor, a transient workforce began to develop. Many individuals, often unemployed or seeking adventure, took to the rails and traveled as itinerant workers.

2. Late 19th to Early 20th Century: During this period, the term "hobo" became more widely used to describe these transient workers who rode freight trains in search of employment. Hobos had their own subculture, including a code of ethics and symbols they would use to communicate with one another. They often lived in camps known as "hobo jungles."

3. Great Depression (1930s): The Great Depression of the 1930s led to a significant increase in the number of homeless and jobless individuals. Many people, including those who had lost their homes and jobs, turned to a life of riding the rails and living as hobos. This period is often considered the peak of hobo culture in the United States.

Hobo culture was a complex phenomenon, and whether it was a voluntary way of life varied from one individual to another. Hoboism encompassed a diverse group of people with different backgrounds, motivations, and circumstances. Here are some key points to consider:

1. Voluntary Choice: For some individuals, becoming a hobo was a voluntary choice. Some people were drawn to the transient lifestyle as a form of adventure, a way to escape societal constraints, or a rejection of conventional norms. They saw it as an opportunity to live a freer and more independent life on the road.

2. Economic Necessity: Many individuals who became hobos did so out of economic necessity. During periods of economic hardship, such as the Great Depression, unemployment and poverty forced people to hit the rails in search of work and food. For them, being a hobo was a response to dire circumstances.

3. Cultural and Subcultural Aspects: Hobo culture had its own set of customs, ethics, and codes. Some individuals were drawn to the camaraderie and sense of community among hobos. They embraced the culture as a way of life that provided social connections and support.

4. Mix of Voluntary and Involuntary: The distinction between voluntary and involuntary hoboism can be blurred. Some people may have initially chosen the lifestyle voluntarily but later found themselves trapped in a cycle of poverty and transience, making it difficult to escape.

5. Regional and Historical Factors: The prevalence and reasons for becoming a hobo could also vary by region and time period. The Dust Bowl era, for example, saw a significant influx of people forced to become hobos due to agricultural devastation and drought.

American Bohemians (1880-1930)

The older I get, the more I tend to conflate the American Bohemian sensibility with Larry Darrell's choice to chuck it all and go a-roaming. American and Parisian Bohemians were contemporaneous, with both movements flourishing during the late 19th and early 20th centuries. While they were distinct in their specific cultural and geographic contexts, they shared many similarities in their rejection of bourgeois values and their pursuit of unconventional, artistic, and nonconformist lifestyles. Certainly Larry was just an offshoot of what must have been a very noticeable sub-culture in Paris.

This reasoning offers a disservice to both parties, as there are some majour differences between, as you will find mentioned in "The Razor's Edge", itself, the wolf that runs with the pack and the lone wolf.

American Bohemians were a diverse group of artists, writers, intellectuals, and free spirits who emerged during the late 19th and early 20th centuries. They rejected conventional social norms and values and sought to create alternative lifestyles characterized by nonconformity, creativity, and a disdain for bourgeois (middle-class) society.

Here are some defining characteristics of American Bohemians during this period:

1. Nonconformity: Bohemians rejected the conformist values of mainstream society. They often questioned the traditional roles assigned to them based on gender, class, and ethnicity.

2. Artistic and Intellectual Pursuits: Many Bohemians were artists, writers, and intellectuals who valued creative expression and intellectual exploration. They often congregated in urban centers, such as New York's Greenwich Village, to collaborate and exchange ideas.

3. Anti-Materialism: Bohemians tended to reject materialism and consumerism. They often lived in modest conditions, emphasizing the pursuit of art, literature, and personal growth over material possessions.

4. Alternative Lifestyles: Bohemians embraced unconventional lifestyles, including communal living, experimentation with new forms of art and literature, and open-minded attitudes toward sexuality.

5. Cultural and Social Critique: They often critiqued the established norms of their time, including societal constraints on freedom of expression, gender roles, and social injustice.

American Bohemians included Djuna Barnes, Man Ray, Eugene O'Neill, Edna St. Vincent Millay, E. E. Cummings, Hart Crane, John Reed, Mabel Dodge Luhan, Langston Hughes and Scott Fitzgerald.

Contrasting Larry Darrell with the American Bohemian

Larry Darrell, the protagonist of W. Somerset Maugham's novel "The Razor's Edge," represents a different kind of individualism and nonconformity compared to the American Bohemians of the early 20th century. While there may be some overlap in their rejection of bourgeois values, Larry's journey is distinctive in several ways:

1. Spiritual Quest: Larry's departure from bourgeois society is primarily driven by a spiritual quest for enlightenment and self-discovery. His experiences in World War I lead him to question the shallow pursuits of material success and prompt him to seek a deeper, more meaningful existence.

2. Ascetic Lifestyle: Unlike some Bohemians who rejected societal norms but still embraced artistic or intellectual pursuits, Larry adopts a more ascetic lifestyle. He travels to India and spends years in contemplation and meditation in pursuit of higher spiritual truths.

3. Personal Transformation: Larry's journey is deeply personal and inward-focused. He seeks to transform himself, overcome his inner conflicts, and attain a state of inner peace and enlightenment. This contrasts with Bohemians, who often sought collective change and cultural critique.

4. Global Perspective: Larry's quest takes him to various parts of the world, including India, where he encounters Eastern spirituality. In contrast, American Bohemians were more centered on urban hubs in the United States.

So, while American Bohemians of the late 19th and early 20th centuries rejected bourgeois society in pursuit of artistic and intellectual freedom, Larry Darrell's departure from that society in "The Razor's Edge" is primarily driven by a personal and spiritual quest for meaning and enlightenment. His journey is more introspective and transcendent in nature.

But Larry's story revolves around the people in Paris, off which he was one for at least a part of the tale. Perhaps he is an offshoot of the Paris Bohemian tree.

Parisian Bohemians (1880-1930)

Parisian Bohemians and American Bohemians, while sharing some common ideals of nonconformity and artistic expression, had distinct characteristics due to their different cultural and historical contexts. Larry Darrell, the protagonist of "The Razor's Edge," does not fit neatly into either category. Here's how Parisian and American Bohemians differed, and why Larry is not considered a typical Bohemian:

Differences Between Parisian and American Bohemians

1. Geographic Location: Parisian Bohemians were centered in the cultural hub of Paris, while American Bohemians had their cultural centers in cities like New York, Chicago, and San Francisco. Different geographic locations influenced the specific characteristics and cultural influences of each Bohemian movement.

2. Cultural Influences: Parisian Bohemians were influenced by the broader European Bohemian tradition, with connections to movements like Impressionism and Symbolism. American Bohemians, on the other hand, reflected American cultural and social trends, including aspects of the counterculture and Beat Generation.

3. Artistic Styles: Parisian Bohemians were associated with avant-garde art movements, including Post-Impressionism and Cubism. American Bohemians contributed to American literary and artistic movements such as the Beat Generation and the Harlem Renaissance.

4. Cultural Impact: Parisian Bohemianism had a significant impact on European art, literature, and culture, particularly during the Belle Époque and the early 20th century. American Bohemianism contributed to the development of American literary and artistic movements and the counterculture of the 1960s.

Why Larry Darrell Can Not Be Considered a Typical Parisian Bohemian

In the 1920s, the Parisian Bohemian community was characterized by its vibrant intellectual and artistic interests. Figures like Gertrude Stein, F. Scott Fitzgerald, and Ernest Hemingway congregated in the city's cultural hubs, such as Montparnasse and Montmartre. They were deeply immersed in literary and artistic experimentation, engaging in the creation of innovative works and the exchange of radical ideas. Their interests were primarily artistic and group-oriented, with a focus on modernist literature and art movements like Surrealism, Dadaism, and the Lost Generation.

Larry Darrell, on the other hand, represented a different intellectual and spiritual trajectory during the same era. His interests extended beyond the artistic and group-oriented pursuits of the Parisian Bohemians. Larry's primary focus was on a profound spiritual quest for meaning and enlightenment, which led him to travel to places like India and engage in practices like meditation and introspection. While the Parisian Bohemians were engaged in artistic revolution and challenging societal norms, Larry was on an introspective journey of self-discovery and personal transformation, seeking a deeper understanding of the self and the universe.

In essence, the contrast lies in the Parisian Bohemians' artistic and group-oriented interests versus Larry's individualistic and spiritually oriented pursuits during the 1920s. While both were nonconformists in their own right, their motivations and areas of exploration differed significantly.

PARIS 1920s

It should be noted that while Bohemian culture did not start in Paris *per se*, Paris was a significant epicenter of this cultural movement in the late 19th and early 20th centuries, and it played a crucial role in shaping and popularizing the Bohemian lifestyle and ethos.

NYC 1920s

Amidst the skyscrapers and bustling streets, downtown Manhattan in the Roaring Twenties epitomized the Jazz Age's exuberance. A city pulsating with the rhythms of jazz, it stood as a beacon of liberation after World War I, only to face the stark realities of the Great Depression in the years to come.

Cultural Landscape Facing Americans Immediately After WW1

After taking a long look at the counter-cultures to which Larry did not belong, we should note a few of the majour cultural shifts, fits, rifts and drifts that must have touched his consciousness during the years covered in the novel, though only the last plays an important role in the narrative.

The cultural landscape of the United States immediately after World War I, often referred to as the Roaring Twenties or the Jazz Age, underwent significant transformations in various aspects, including music, fashion, literature, and social attitudes.

1. Jazz and Music: The Roaring Twenties was marked by the emergence of jazz as a dominant cultural force. Jazz music, characterized by its lively rhythms and improvisation, became synonymous with the era and had a profound influence on American culture. Iconic jazz figures like Louis Armstrong and Duke Ellington gained prominence, and jazz clubs thrived in cities like New Orleans, Chicago, and New York.

2. Flappers and Fashion: The 1920s saw a dramatic shift in fashion, with the "flapper" style becoming iconic. Flappers were young women who rejected traditional gender norms, wearing short skirts, bobbed hair, and adopting a more liberated lifestyle. The "garçonne" look, characterized by its boyish and androgynous appearance, challenged conventional standards of femininity.

3. Literature and the Lost Generation: American literature during this period was deeply influenced by the experiences of World War I and the disillusionment that followed. The "Lost Generation" of writers, including F. Scott Fitzgerald, Ernest Hemingway, and Gertrude Stein, explored themes of alienation, moral bankruptcy, and the search for meaning in a post-war world. Fitzgerald's "The Great Gatsby" is often considered a quintessential novel of this era.

4. Cinema and Hollywood: The 1920s marked the golden age of silent film, with Hollywood becoming the epicenter of the global film industry. Stars like Charlie Chaplin and Rudolph Valentino achieved international fame. The era also saw the transition from silent films to "talkies" with the release of "The Jazz Singer" in 1927.

5. Prohibition and Speakeasies: Prohibition, the nationwide ban on the sale and consumption of alcoholic beverages, was in effect from 1920 to 1933. This led to the rise of illegal bars and clubs known as speakeasies, where patrons could drink and socialize covertly. The era is often associated with gangsters like Al Capone and organized crime.

6. Social Change and Women's Suffrage: The 1920s brought significant social changes, including the ratification of the 19th Amendment in 1920, granting women the right to vote. Women's roles in society began to shift, and they became increasingly visible in the workforce, politics, and public life.

7. Consumer Culture: The 1920s saw the rise of consumer culture, with a surge in the availability of consumer goods, including automobiles, radios, and household appliances. Advertising and marketing became integral to American life, promoting the idea of the "good life" through consumption.

8. Social Liberalization: While the decade had its share of cultural conservatism, it also witnessed a degree of social liberalization, including discussions about sexual freedom, birth control, and women's reproductive rights.

9. Art Deco and Architecture: The Art Deco style, characterized by geometric designs and luxurious materials, influenced architecture and design during the 1920s. Skyscrapers, such as the Empire State Building, showcased this architectural style.

10. The Ex-Pat Culture in Paris: After World War I, American expatriates flocked to Paris for its cultural allure, artistic vibrancy, and post-war liberation. The city offered a haven for creative souls seeking to escape wartime trauma, indulge in a bohemian lifestyle, and find inspiration, all at a relatively affordable cost of living due to favorable exchange rates.

In short, the cultural landscape of the United States immediately after World War I was a period of profound transformation, marked by cultural innovation, social change, and a spirit of both rebellion and celebration. The Roaring Twenties captured the dynamism and complexity of an era that sought to redefine American identity in the aftermath of a devastating global conflict.

Week 1:
Introduction to Self-Actualization vs. Self-Delusion

The Course Overview

Course Description:

This course explores the themes of self-actualization and self-delusion as they manifest in American life through the lens of Somerset Maugham's classic novel, "The Razor's Edge." Through a deep dive into the novel and related texts, students will critically examine the pursuit of meaning, authenticity, and fulfillment in the context of 20th-century America. By analyzing the characters and their journeys in "The Razor's Edge," students will gain insight into the complexities of self-discovery, societal expectations, and the American Dream.

Course Objectives:

1. Understand the Concept of Self-Actualization:
- Define and explore the concept of self-actualization.
- Identify key characteristics and traits of self-actualized individuals.
- Examine the relevance of self-actualization in the context of American culture and society.

2. Analyze Somerset Maugham's "The Razor's Edge":
- Read and interpret the novel "The Razor's Edge" in depth.
- Analyze the characters' quests for self-actualization and their varying degrees of success.
- Discuss the cultural and societal factors that influence the characters' decisions and paths.

3. Compare Self-Actualization and Self-Delusion:
- Explore the fine line between self-actualization and self-delusion.
- Discuss instances in the novel where characters teeter on the edge of these two states.
- Analyze how societal pressures and personal motivations contribute to self-delusion.

4. Examine the American Dream:

- Investigate the concept of the American Dream and its evolving definitions.
- Discuss how characters in "The Razor's Edge" pursue or challenge the American Dream.
- Reflect on the role of materialism and social status in the characters' lives.

5. Engage with Supplementary Texts:

- Read and analyze supplementary texts, including essays, articles, and contemporary works, related to self-actualization, American culture, and societal expectations.
- Compare and contrast the themes in "The Razor's Edge" with those in other literary and non-literary sources.

6. Critical Thinking and Discussion:

- Encourage critical thinking through class discussions and written assignments.
- Foster an environment where students can articulate and defend their interpretations of the text.
- Engage in debates on the characters' choices and the consequences of self-actualization and self-delusion.

7. Final Project:

- Culminate the course with a final project that allows students to delve deeper into a specific aspect of the novel, its themes, or related topics.
- Present findings through essays, presentations, or creative projects that demonstrate a comprehensive understanding of the course material.
- Of course, not everyone reading this book will need to present a final project. Perhaps thinking on the Core text every so often would be enough to make this journey worthwhile.

By the end of this course, students will have gained a nuanced understanding of the contrasting paths of self-actualization and self-delusion in American life, as portrayed in Somerset Maugham's "The Razor's Edge." They will also be equipped with the critical thinking skills necessary to analyze and interpret complex literary works and their socio-cultural implications.

§

The American Dream and Its Manifestations from the 1700s to the 1930s

1. Colonial America (1700s):

The American Dream's early roots can be traced back to the colonial period when settlers sought religious freedom, economic opportunities, and land ownership.

Manifestations included the pursuit of religious freedom in colonies like Massachusetts, the quest for economic prosperity through trade and agriculture, and the desire for personal autonomy and self-sufficiency.

2. The Revolutionary Era (1770s):

The American Dream gained momentum during the Revolutionary era as colonists fought for independence from British rule.

Manifestations included the belief in individual liberty and the idea that hard work and determination could lead to social mobility and a better life.

Thomas Paine's writings, like "Common Sense," emphasized the idea of a democratic society where citizens had the opportunity to shape their own destinies.

3. Westward Expansion (Early 1800s):

The 19th century saw the expansion of the American Dream westward, with the frontier representing opportunities for land ownership and economic prosperity.

Manifestations included the Homestead Act of 1862, which offered free land to settlers willing to develop it, and the Gold Rushes, where people sought wealth and fortune in the West.

4. Industrialization and Immigration (Late 1800s):
The late 19th century brought industrialization and a surge in immigration, leading to new manifestations of the American Dream.

Manifestations included the pursuit of upward mobility through hard work and industrial employment, as well as the idea that anyone, regardless of background, could achieve success in America.

5. The Gilded Age (Late 1800s to Early 1900s):
During the Gilded Age, the American Dream was often associated with material success, particularly for the wealthy elite.

Manifestations included conspicuous consumption, the rise of industrial barons, and the belief in social Darwinism, where success was seen as a sign of personal virtue.

6. The Progressive Era (Early 1900s):
The Progressive Era brought a critique of the excesses of the Gilded Age and a reexamination of the American Dream.

Manifestations included social and political reforms aimed at reducing inequality and ensuring equal opportunities for all, such as labor rights, women's suffrage, and trust-busting.

7. The Great Depression (1930s):
The economic devastation of the Great Depression challenged the traditional manifestations of the American Dream.

Manifestations included a struggle for survival, a reevaluation of materialism, and government intervention through New Deal programs aimed at providing relief and economic stability.

Throughout these periods, the American Dream evolved and adapted to the changing social, economic, and political landscape of the United States. It continued to represent the aspirations of individuals and communities, even as its manifestations shifted from land ownership and economic prosperity to broader ideals of liberty, equality, and social justice.

The Concept of Self-Actualization and Self-Delusion in the U.S. from the 1700s to the 1930s

Introduction

Throughout American history, individuals grappled with societal constraints and the seductive allure of unattainable dreams.

From colonial struggles for identity to the Great Depression's disillusionment, these themes recurred. This essay will explore these dynamics, shedding light on the human condition across centuries of American experience.

I. Colonial America: Religious Conformity and Self-Delusion (1700s)

In Colonial America, a fervent desire for religious freedom was held back by rigid societal expectations. While some sought self-actualization through faith, others were closed off from this path by the oppressive dogma of their communities, leading to self-delusion as they convinced themselves of conformity.

II. Revolutionary Era: Aspirations vs. Reality (1770s)

Despite the ideal of individual liberty during the Revolutionary Era, not everyone could partake. Slavery, discrimination, and economic constraints denied many their path to self-actualization. Meanwhile, the dream of revolution, while inspiring, sometimes led to the delusion that freedom was attainable for all.

III. Westward Expansion: Displacement and the Illusion of the Frontier (Early 1800s)

The allure of westward expansion promised land and opportunity, but it also led to the displacement and suffering of indigenous communities. Manifest Destiny, a 19th-century belief in American expansion, wasn't embraced by all. Critics saw it as morally troubling, leading to the forced removal of Native Americans, Mexican-American War, and annexation debates. It underscored a complex tension between territorial ambition and ethical concerns within the nation's expansionist narrative.

IV. Industrialization: Labor Exploitation and the Mirage of Wealth (Late 1800s)

Industrialization brought immense wealth to a few, but it was built on the exploitation of workers. While 19th-century industrialization in the United States brought unprecedented economic growth and innovation, it did not ensure freedom and prosperity for all. Many laborers endured harsh working conditions, long hours, and low wages in factories and mines. Child labor was rampant, and workplace safety was minimal, resulting in accidents and health issues. Urbanization led to overcrowded, unsanitary living conditions in tenements. Meanwhile, women and minority groups faced systemic discrimination and limited opportunities. Industrialization's benefits were often unequally distributed, creating stark inequalities and social injustices, challenging the notion that it universally brought freedom and prosperity to all Americans during that era.

V. The Gilded Age: Materialism and Hollow Success (Late 1800s to Early 1900s)

The Gilded Age in late 19th century America was marked by remarkable economic growth and industrialization, yet it also brought forth a sense of spiritual emptiness. As society rapidly modernized and embraced materialism, many individuals experienced a profound disconnect from deeper spiritual values and meaning in their lives. The relentless pursuit of wealth, consumerism, and urbanization left many feeling spiritually adrift.

In response to this void, there was a simultaneous rise in various forms of spiritual and religious expression. Spiritualism, for instance, gained traction as people sought solace and reassurance in connecting with the spiritual realm, often through mediums who claimed to communicate with the deceased.

Additionally, new religious movements and intentional communities emerged, such as the Oneida Community and the Shakers. These communities provided alternative spaces for spiritual exploration and communal living outside the confines of mainstream religions.

Moreover, the period saw a resurgence of religious fervor with the Great Awakening, a series of religious revivals that swept across the nation. It offered individuals a sense of purpose and revivalist zeal, addressing the perceived moral decline of the era and providing a spiritual outlet.

In essence, the spiritual emptiness of the Gilded Age prompted a multifaceted response, encompassing spiritualism, new religious communities, and religious revivals, as people sought to fill the void and rediscover deeper spiritual meaning amidst the rapid changes of their time.

VI. The Progressive Era: Inequality and Reform (Early 1900s)

In the Progressive Era, the glaring inequalities of the Gilded Age spurred calls for reform. Still, entrenched interests and societal norms created barriers to genuine self-actualization for marginalized groups. Those who supported reform believed they were actualizing the American Dream of justice, but the dream remained elusive for many.

VII. The Great Depression: Struggle for Survival and FDR's New Deal (1930s)

During the Great Depression of the 1930s, American religious life underwent a significant transformation in response to the economic turmoil and social upheaval. Many individuals turned to faith for solace and hope in the face of widespread unemployment and poverty.

Churches, synagogues, and mosques provided spiritual comfort and a sense of community support. Concurrently, religious communities engaged in social activism, advocating for economic reforms and social welfare, aligning faith with social justice causes. The era witnessed the rise of religious radio programs that reached millions of listeners, combining religious messages with economic and political commentary.

Diverse religious responses emerged, from the Social Gospel movement's focus on addressing social injustices to the growth of charismatic Christianity, reflecting the nation's religious diversity.

American religious life during the Great Depression became a dynamic space where faith, social action, and coping mechanisms converged, highlighting the resilience of religious institutions in addressing the era's pressing challenges.

§

The tension between aspiration and reality, between the promise of the American Dream and its often-elusive nature, remains a central theme in the nation's story.

Throughout American history from the 1700s to the 1930s, the ability to reach for self-actualization was often influenced by various factors, including social class, race, gender, and access to education and opportunities.

Here's an overview of who could and could not easily pursue self-actualization during this period:

Who Could Reach for Self-Actualization:

1. White Men of Privilege: White men from affluent backgrounds generally had the most access to education, opportunities, and resources, allowing them to pursue self-actualization through careers, entrepreneurship, and intellectual pursuits.

2. Educated Middle Class: The educated middle class, including professionals, businessmen, and some women, had better opportunities for self-actualization, particularly in urban centers, where they could engage in various intellectual and creative endeavors.

3. Intellectuals and Artists: Individuals with artistic talents, writers, and intellectuals could pursue self-actualization through their creative expressions, although success often depended on societal acceptance and patronage.

4. Select Women's Rights Advocates: Women who were pioneers in the women's suffrage and feminist movements made strides toward self-actualization by advocating for gender equality and expanded opportunities for women.

Who Could Not Easily Reach for Self-Actualization:

1. Enslaved and Free Black Americans: Black Americans, whether enslaved or free, faced systemic racism and discrimination, limiting their access to education, employment, and self-actualization opportunities.

2. Indigenous Peoples: Native Americans were marginalized, forcibly relocated, and had their cultures suppressed, severely limiting their ability to pursue self-actualization on their own terms.

3. Working Class: The working-class majority often had limited educational opportunities and faced harsh working conditions, leaving them with little time or resources for self-actualization beyond basic survival.

4. Women's Limited Rights: For much of this period, women faced legal and societal restrictions on their rights and opportunities, particularly in terms of education and career choices.

5. Immigrant Populations: Immigrants, especially those from non-European backgrounds, faced discrimination and economic challenges that hindered their pursuit of self-actualization.

Self-actualization in American society from the 1700s to the 1930s was significantly influenced by social factors, privilege, and access to opportunities. White men of privilege and the educated middle class had more avenues for self-actualization, while marginalized groups such as Black Americans, Indigenous peoples, and women faced significant barriers to achieving their full potential.

While each of these eras and each of these cultural conflicts are subjects worthy of deep and continuing study, here they are meant to provide historical context for the conflicts the characters face in the novel.

It should also be noted that Maslow's Hierarchy of Needs has a great deal to with who gets to reach for ultimate purposes and who just grinds out the days. Larry Darrell's quest is of interest because he voluntarily forgoes several basic needs to dedicate himself to higher needs.

Week 2:
W. Somerset Maugham and The Razor's Edge

W. Somerset Maugham

W. Somerset Maugham: A Literary Journey through Life and Works

William Somerset Maugham, a prolific British author, playwright, and novelist, left an indelible mark on 20th-century literature. Born on January 25, 1874, in Paris, France, to British parents, Maugham's early life was marked by adversity and personal challenges, which profoundly influenced his literary career. Over the course of his long and fruitful life, Maugham penned numerous novels, short stories, and plays that captivated readers and audiences alike, earning him a reputation as one of the most successful and enduring literary figures of his time.

Maugham's early years were marked by tragedy and loss. His parents died when he was a child, leaving him orphaned and in the care of his uncle. This sense of abandonment and early exposure to hardship served as a recurring theme in his works, where characters often grapple with their own trials and tribulations. Maugham's experiences as a medical student in London further informed his writing, as he was exposed to the complexities of human nature and the human condition, which would become central themes in his literary works.

One of Maugham's most famous novels, "Of Human Bondage," published in 1915, draws heavily from his own experiences as a medical student. The novel chronicles the life of Philip Carey, a young man who, like Maugham, pursues a career in medicine but faces numerous personal challenges and romantic entanglements. The novel delves into themes of self-discovery, unrequited love, and the pursuit of one's true passion, making it a poignant reflection of Maugham's own struggles and aspirations.

Maugham's writing style is often characterized by its clarity, simplicity, and keen observational skills. He had a knack for dissecting human emotions and motivations, presenting them in a lucid and accessible manner. This style appealed to a wide range of readers and contributed to the enduring popularity of his works.

In addition to his novels, Maugham was a prolific short story writer. His short stories, collected in volumes such as "The Trembling of a Leaf" and "Rain and Other South Sea Stories," showcase his talent for crafting compelling narratives within a limited space. Many of his short stories are set in exotic locales, reflecting his own extensive travels.

Maugham's love for travel and exploration played a significant role in both his life and his writing. He traveled extensively throughout his lifetime, visiting countries such as India, the United States, and the South Pacific. These journeys provided him with a wealth of material and inspiration for his stories. His experiences in colonial Malaya, for instance, inspired his novel "The Painted Veil," which explores themes of love, infidelity, and redemption in a foreign land.

Among Maugham's most enduring works is "The Razor's Edge," published in 1944. The novel tells the story of Larry Darrell, a disillusioned World War I veteran who embarks on a spiritual quest to find meaning in life. This departure from Maugham's usual themes of social satire and personal drama marked a significant evolution in his writing. "The Razor's Edge" delves into themes of Eastern philosophy, spirituality, and the search for enlightenment, reflecting Maugham's own interest in these subjects.

Maugham's career was not confined to the realm of literature alone; he was also a successful playwright. His plays, such as "The Circle" and "Our Betters," enjoyed considerable success on both sides of the Atlantic. His ability to craft witty and socially astute dialogue made him a prominent figure in the theater world.

Despite his achievements, Maugham faced criticism from some quarters for his conservative views and perceived lack of experimentation in his writing. However, his steadfast commitment to storytelling that resonated with a broad readership contributed to his lasting popularity and literary influence.

In his later years, Maugham settled in the south of France, where he continued to write and enjoy a life of relative seclusion. He passed away on December 16, 1965, leaving behind a rich literary legacy that continues to be celebrated and studied.

W. Somerset Maugham's life and works are a testament to the enduring power of storytelling. Through his novels, short stories, and plays, he explored the complexities of human nature, the pursuit of happiness, and the enduring search for meaning in a world marked by adversity and uncertainty. His ability to connect with readers on a profound level, coupled with his gift for storytelling, ensures that his works remain relevant and beloved by generations of readers and scholars alike. Somerset Maugham's life and works are a testament to the enduring power of storytelling. Through his novels, short stories, and plays, he explored the complexities of human nature, the pursuit of happiness, and the enduring search for meaning in a world marked by adversity and uncertainty. His ability to connect with readers on a profound level, coupled with his gift for storytelling, ensures that his works remain relevant and beloved by generations of readers and scholars alike.

§

One notable anecdote related to W. Somerset Maugham and "The Razor's Edge" involves his inspiration for the character of Larry Darrell, the novel's protagonist.

Maugham was a well-known writer and playwright in the early 20th century, and his own experiences often influenced his fictional works. While traveling in the United States in the 1920s, he met a young American named Gerald Haxton. Haxton, who was openly gay, became Maugham's companion and secretary for many years.

Gerald Haxton's personality and life choices greatly influenced Maugham. Haxton's quest for a more meaningful and unconventional life, as well as his interest in Eastern spirituality, provided inspiration for the character of Larry Darrell in "The Razor's Edge." Larry's journey of self-discovery and his exploration of Eastern philosophy and mysticism echo the experiences and interests of Haxton.

Week 2: Historical Context: Post-World War I America

The Never-Ending Fire

Post-World War I America, up to and just after the Great Depression, was a period of significant historical and cultural change. Here are 10 important features that characterized this era:

1. Roaring Twenties: The decade began with a post-World War I economic boom, and many people experienced increased prosperity. The stock market soared, and consumerism thrived as more people gained access to goods and services.

The 1920s were known as the Roaring Twenties due to the exuberant atmosphere of economic prosperity and cultural dynamism. It was a time of jazz music, flapper fashion, and a general sense of celebration. The effects of this exuberance and joy fading into nothing effected everything and everyone.

2. Prohibition: The 18th Amendment to the U.S. Constitution enacted Prohibition, making the manufacture and sale of alcoholic beverages illegal. This led to the rise of speakeasies and organized crime, and government corruption.

The era led to the popularization of mixed drinks and cocktails, as bartenders and patrons sought creative ways to mask the taste of poorly made or unsafe bootlegged liquor.

And, Prohibition also gave rise to cultural resistance against government regulation, reflecting a desire for personal freedom and the right to make one's own choices.

3. Women's Suffrage: The 19th Amendment, ratified in 1920, granted women the right to vote nationwide, marking a significant victory for the women's suffrage movement. Victory did not visit without sacrifice.

In 1913, Washington, D.C., the Women's Suffrage Parade organized by Alice Paul and the National American Woman Suffrage Association (NAWSA) faced hostility and violence from anti-suffrage groups and onlookers. Some participants were physically attacked and subjected to verbal abuse.

In 1917, The Night of Terror: Suffragists, including Alice Paul and Lucy Burns, were imprisoned at the Occoquan Workhouse in Virginia for their protest activities. They endured harsh treatment and a brutal night of abuse from prison guards, which became known as the "Night of Terror."

This was not an easy victory for universal human rights and certainly influenced the choices available to the female characters we will soon be taking a closer look at in the following weeks.

4. The Jazz Age: Jazz music became a defining cultural element of the era, with prominent musicians like Louis Armstrong and Duke Ellington. Jazz represented the spirit of the age, emphasizing improvisation and rhythm.

In Paris, the Jazz Age was also a prominent cultural phenomenon during the 1920s. The city became a hub for American expatriates, writers, artists, and musicians who flocked to its vibrant cultural scene. Parisian cafes and nightclubs, such as the famous Le Moulin Rouge, were venues where jazz music thrived, and they played a vital role in popularizing the genre in Europe.

5. Cultural Modernism: The 1920s saw a flourishing of modernist literature, art, and architecture. Writers like F. Scott Fitzgerald and Ernest Hemingway, along with artists like Georgia O'Keeffe, made significant contributions.

6. The Great Migration: African Americans from the rural South moved to Northern cities during this period, seeking economic opportunities and escaping racial discrimination. This migration had a profound impact on urban culture.

7. Stock Market Boom and Crash: The stock market experienced rapid growth during the 1920s, culminating in the Wall Street Crash of 1929. The crash marked the beginning of the Great Depression. 8. Dust Bowl: Environmental factors, including drought and soil erosion, led to the Dust Bowl in the Southern Plains, causing agricultural devastation and mass migration of farmers.

8. Dust Bowl: Environmental factors, including drought and soil erosion, led to the Dust Bowl in the Southern Plains, causing agricultural devastation and mass migration of farmers from 1931-1939.

9. New Deal: President Franklin D. Roosevelt's New Deal programs aimed to address the economic challenges of the Great Depression. These initiatives included Social Security, public works projects, and financial regulations.

10. Literature and Art of the Great Depression: The cultural response to the Great Depression included literature such as John Steinbeck's "The Grapes of Wrath" and art projects like the Works Progress Administration (WPA), which employed artists to create public art.

This era represents a transitional period in American history, marked by both cultural innovation and economic hardship, as the nation grappled with the aftermath of World War I and the challenges of the Great Depression.

§

Week 2: Overview of The Razor's Edge. The Novel.

"The Razor's Edge," a novel by W. Somerset Maugham published in 1944, tells the story of Larry Darrell's quest for meaning and self-discovery in the aftermath of World War I. The novel's enduring appeal can be attributed to its timeless exploration of universal themes, rich character development, and the thought-provoking journey of its protagonist.

Plot Summary:

"The Razor's Edge" is set in the years following World War I and primarily takes place in Chicago, Paris, and India. The novel begins with a group of friends in Chicago, including the protagonist, Larry Darrell, and his fiancée, Isabel Bradley. Larry, a young and promising pilot, returns from the war deeply affected by the horrors he witnessed. He becomes disillusioned with materialism and seeks a deeper understanding of life's purpose.

As Larry embarks on his spiritual journey, he parts ways with Isabel, who desires a more conventional and affluent life. Isabel marries another man, Gray Maturin, who represents the pursuit of wealth and social status. Meanwhile, Larry travels to Paris and then to India, where he immerses himself in Eastern philosophy and spirituality. He studies under a guru and renounces materialism in favor of a life devoted to self-realization.

The novel also follows the lives of other characters affected by Larry's choices. Maugham, who serves as the narrator, shares his observations of Larry's journey and its impact on those around him. This includes the struggles and personal transformations of characters like Sophie MacDonald, a troubled young woman, and Elliott Templeton, a socialite who epitomizes the superficial values Larry rejects.

Throughout the novel, Maugham's narrative skillfully weaves together the diverse experiences and perspectives of the characters, highlighting the contrast between materialism and the pursuit of inner truth.

Why "The Razor's Edge" Stands the Test of Time

1. Timeless Themes: "The Razor's Edge" explores enduring themes that resonate with readers across generations. Larry Darrell's quest for meaning, the tension between materialism and spirituality, and the search for authenticity are universal concerns that continue to be relevant in contemporary society.

2. Complex Characters: Maugham's characters are multi-dimensional and relatable. Readers can empathize with their struggles, growth, and inner conflicts. Larry Darrell's transformation from a disillusioned war veteran to a spiritual seeker is a compelling character arc.

3. Rich Cultural Context: The novel offers a vivid portrayal of the post-World War I era, capturing the cultural shifts and societal changes of the time. From the decadence of the Jazz Age to the allure of Eastern mysticism, the story immerses readers in the cultural tapestry of the early 20th century.

4. Philosophical Exploration: "The Razor's Edge" delves into philosophical and existential questions about the nature of life, happiness, and the pursuit of truth. Larry's spiritual journey serves as a lens through which these profound questions are examined.

5. Narrative Style: Maugham's narrative style, in which he serves as both a character in the story and the storyteller, provides a unique perspective on the events. His introspective and observant narration adds depth to the narrative.

6. Relevance to Different Ages: The novel's themes of self-discovery and the search for meaning are timeless and can resonate with readers at various stages of life, making it accessible and thought-provoking for both young and mature audiences.

"The Razor's Edge" continues to stand the test of time due to its exploration of enduring themes, well-crafted characters, and its ability to provoke introspection and contemplation. Larry Darrell's journey of self-discovery remains a compelling and inspirational narrative that transcends its original context and speaks to the human condition.

Week 3:
The Protagonists in Depth

note:
this week can easily be broken up into two or three weeks

Week 3: Characters in Depth- Characters in Conflict

In "The Razor's Edge" by Somerset Maugham, there are American characters whose uniquely American traits clash or coexist with European and, in Larry's case, South-East Asian standards, norms, and archetypes.

Here's an analysis of the American characters and their interactions with different cultural norms:

Larry Darrell:

Uniquely American Traits: Larry embodies the American spirit of individualism and self-determination. He rejects societal norms and materialism in favor of a personal quest for truth and self-realization. His willingness to explore Eastern spirituality represents the American openness to diverse philosophies and spiritual paths.

Clash and Coexistence: Larry's rejection of materialism clashes with the European and, to some extent, American norms of the 1920s, which were marked by excess and a pursuit of social status. In South-East Asia, he seeks spiritual wisdom that contrasts with Western Christianity but aligns with Eastern spirituality.

Isabel Bradley:

Uniquely American Traits: Isabel initially embodies the American dream of upward mobility and social success. She values social status, ambition, and adherence to societal norms, which were common traits associated with the American middle and upper classes during the Jazz Age.

Clash and Coexistence: Isabel's pursuit of conventional success and her desire for stability and social status clash with Larry's rejection of these values. This conflict illustrates the tension between American ideals of material success and individualism versus Larry's quest for spiritual fulfillment.

Elliott Templeton:

Uniquely American Traits: Elliott embodies the American fascination with European high society. He values social connections, cultural refinement, and adherence to European aristocratic norms. His character reflects the American desire for acceptance and recognition within European elite circles.

Clash and Coexistence: Elliott's American background, combined with his European aspirations, leads to a complex coexistence of American and European norms. He is accepted in European high society but still perceives himself as an American striving for recognition in a foreign cultural context.

Sophie is British.

Sophie MacDonald:

Uniquely British Traits: Sophie initially expresses many British traits of her time, including reserve and politeness, social class awareness, emotional restraint, societal expectations, British Stoicism and repect for a famliy which she loses.

Clash and Coexistence: Sophie's character faces significant tragedy, including the loss of her husband in World War I and the death of her child. Her struggles with addiction and emotional instability contribute to her tragic arc.

Her character serves as a bridge between these conflicting values, embodying the tension between conformity and nonconformity, materialism and spiritualism, and societal expectations and personal liberation.

Each character's personal journey contributes to the overarching themes of the novel, which revolve around the search for meaning and the quest for a more fulfilling life.

Week 3: Characters in Depth- Larry Darrell

Larry Darrell's character arc in "The Razor's Edge" begins with disillusionment after World War I, leading him to reject materialism. He embarks on a spiritual quest, studying in India and seeking self-realization. His transformation represents a profound shift from societal expectations to a pursuit of inner truth and authenticity.

Larry Darrell's quest for enlightenment in "The Razor's Edge" is influenced by various philosophical and spiritual traditions, including Hinduism and Buddhism, but it differs in some key ways from traditional Eastern and, later, the Beat Generation, which was just starting to emerge at the time "The Razor's Edge" was published, quests for enlightenment. Let's take a closer look.

1. Origin and Cultural Context:

Larry Darrell: Larry's quest for enlightenment is rooted in his personal response to the trauma and disillusionment caused by World War I. He is an American who embarks on a journey of self-discovery and spiritual exploration, drawing inspiration from Eastern philosophies.

Hindu and Buddhist Quests: Hinduism and Buddhism originated in Asia and have deep cultural and religious traditions dating back centuries. The Eastern quests for enlightenment are often deeply ingrained in the cultural fabric of Asian societies.

2. Methods and Practices:

Larry Darrell: Larry's quest involves meditation, contemplation, and seeking the wisdom of spiritual teachers, but it is not bound by strict religious or ritualistic practices. His approach is more individualistic and eclectic.

Hindu and Buddhist Quests: Traditional Eastern paths to enlightenment often involve adherence to specific religious doctrines, rituals, and meditation practices prescribed by their respective traditions.

3. Spiritual Goals:

Larry Darrell: Larry's quest for enlightenment is centered on personal growth, self-realization, and the pursuit of inner truth and meaning. He seeks to transcend the superficial and materialistic aspects of life to find a deeper understanding of existence.

Hindu and Buddhist Quests: Hinduism and Buddhism typically emphasize liberation from the cycle of birth and rebirth (moksha or nirvana) as the ultimate spiritual goal. The focus is on breaking free from the cycle of suffering and achieving a state of transcendence.

4. Social and Cultural Context:

Larry Darrell: Larry's quest takes place in a Western, post-World War I context, where he confronts societal norms and expectations. His journey is often seen as a departure from conventional Western values.

Beat Quests: The Beat Generation, represented by writers like Jack Kerouac and Allen Ginsberg, sought spiritual enlightenment and liberation through travel, experimentation with substances, and a rejection of mainstream American values. Their quest was often characterized by rebellion against societal norms.

While Larry Darrell's quest for enlightenment shares some common themes with Hindu, Buddhist, and Beat quests, such as the search for deeper meaning and self-realization, it is distinct in its cultural context, methods, and spiritual goals. Larry's journey is an individual and unique expression of the universal human longing for spiritual growth and understanding.

Mumbai 1928-1930 (?)

In the late 1920s, Mumbai, known as Bombay during British colonial rule, was a religiously diverse city. It housed vibrant communities of Hindus, Muslims, Christians, Sikhs, and others.

This period witnessed religious festivals, interfaith dialogue, and the coexistence of various faiths, contributing to Mumbai's rich tapestry of religious diversity.

Larry Darrell and the Asian Religious Traditions

Larry Darrell's spiritual quest in Somerset Maugham's "The Razor's Edge" exhibits characteristics that resonate with aspects of Asian spiritual traditions, particularly those influenced by Eastern philosophies. While Larry's journey is not confined to a single tradition, it reflects elements of Eastern spirituality and is informed by various religions and philosophies. Here are ways in which Larry's story exemplifies an "Asian" spiritual quest:

1. Quest for Self-Realization: Larry's primary motivation is to discover his true self and attain self-realization. This is a fundamental theme in many Eastern spiritual traditions, such as Buddhism and Hinduism, which emphasize understanding one's inner nature and transcending the ego.

2. Detachment from Materialism: Larry rejects the pursuit of material success and societal expectations in favor of a simpler, more contemplative lifestyle. This renunciation of materialism is in line with the teachings of Eastern philosophies, where detachment from worldly attachments is often seen as a path to spiritual growth.

3. Meditation and Contemplation: Larry engages in meditation and contemplative practices during his travels, particularly during his time in India. These practices are central to many Asian spiritual traditions, especially within Buddhism and Hinduism, as a means to achieve mindfulness and self-awareness.

4. Influence of Indian Spirituality: Larry's spiritual journey is significantly influenced by his time in India, a country with a rich spiritual heritage. His interactions with Indian gurus and exposure to Eastern philosophies shape his outlook and spiritual practices.

5. Search for Higher Truth: Like many seekers in Asian spiritual traditions, Larry is on a quest for a higher truth or ultimate reality. His journey involves exploring metaphysical and existential questions about the nature of life, suffering, and the self.

6. Rejection of Conventional Religion: Larry's spiritual quest does not align with conventional Western religious practices or dogma. This rejection of organized religion in favor of a more individual and eclectic spiritual path reflects a characteristic of Eastern-influenced spirituality.

7. Egalitarian Perspective: Larry's spiritual journey promotes an egalitarian worldview, valuing all individuals regardless of their social status or background. This perspective aligns with certain Eastern philosophies that emphasize the interconnectedness of all beings.

While Larry's spiritual journey exhibits traits reminiscent of Asian spiritual quests, it's important to note that his path is a fusion of influences from various Eastern and Western traditions, as well as his unique personal experiences. His journey is a testament to the fluidity and adaptability of spirituality, demonstrating that seekers may draw inspiration from diverse sources in their pursuit of self-realization and enlightenment.

Larry Darrell and Hinduism and Buddhism

Larry Darrell's quest and realizations in "The Razor's Edge" align with certain aspects of both Hinduism and Buddhism, although his journey does not adhere strictly to any specific school of thought within these traditions. Here are some ways in which his quest resonates with elements of Hinduism and Buddhism:

Hinduism:

1. Quest for Self-Realization (Atman): In Hinduism, the ultimate goal is often described as self-realization or the understanding of one's true self (Atman). Larry's journey reflects this pursuit as he seeks to discover his inner nature and attain a deeper understanding of himself and the world.

2. Renunciation and Detachment (Vairagya): Hinduism teaches the importance of detachment from material desires and attachments (Vairagya) as a means to achieve spiritual growth. Larry's rejection of materialism and societal expectations aligns with this principle.

3. Meditation and Contemplation (Dhyana): Larry engages in meditation and contemplative practices during his travels, which are common in Hinduism as methods for achieving self-realization and spiritual awakening.

4. Influence of Indian Gurus: Larry's interactions with Indian gurus, particularly with the character Shri Ganesha, reflect the influence of spiritual teachers in Hinduism. Gurus play a crucial role in guiding seekers toward self-realization.

Buddhism:

1. Four Noble Truths: Larry's journey parallels the Four Noble Truths in Buddhism, which identify suffering (dukkha), the cause of suffering (craving and attachment), the possibility of cessation of suffering, and the path (Eightfold Path) to the cessation of suffering. Larry's quest is driven by an awareness of human suffering and a desire to transcend it.

2. Renunciation (Sannyasa): Larry's rejection of a conventional career and material pursuits is akin to the act of renunciation (sannyasa) practiced by Buddhist monks and nuns. Renunciation is a way to detach from worldly desires and attachments.

3. Middle Path: The Middle Path, advocated by Siddhartha Gautama (Buddha), involves avoiding extremes of self-indulgence and self-mortification. Larry's journey embodies a balanced approach, as he seeks meaning and self-realization without resorting to extreme asceticism or hedonism.

4. Mindfulness and Insight (Vipassana): Larry's meditative and contemplative practices align with the Buddhist emphasis on mindfulness (sati) and insight (vipassana) as tools for gaining self-awareness and understanding the nature of reality.

It's important to note that Larry's spiritual journey is not an exact replica of any particular Hindu or Buddhist school of thought but rather draws inspiration from various elements of these traditions. His quest represents a synthesis of Eastern spiritual ideas and his own personal experiences, making it a unique and eclectic spiritual path that resonates with themes of self-realization, renunciation, and mindfulness found in both Hinduism and Buddhism.

Larry Darrell - Issues Related to Syncretism and Appropriation

Larry Darrell's personal spiritual vision in "The Razor's Edge" can be seen as a form of religious syncretism, although it is not a traditional or systematic syncretism.

However, his journey involves the blending of diverse religious and philosophical influences, often in a highly individualistic and eclectic manner.

Defining Religious Syncretism:

Religious syncretism is the merging or blending of different religious beliefs, practices, and traditions into a new, often hybrid, form of spirituality. It involves the reconciliation or incorporation of diverse religious elements to create a unified or harmonious religious system. This process can occur through cultural exchange, interfaith dialogue, or the adaptation of religious practices over time.

With this in mind, let's take a look at Larry's experience and practice.

1. Eclectic Blend: Larry's spiritual quest draws from a wide range of sources, including elements of Hinduism, Buddhism, Christian mysticism, and Western philosophy. He is not bound by the strict adherence to a single tradition but rather integrates what resonates with him personally.

2. Seeking Universal Truth: Larry's primary goal is to seek universal truths and spiritual insights that transcend the boundaries of specific religions. He is not interested in adhering to dogmas or rituals but rather in exploring the core spiritual principles that underpin various faiths.

3. Personal Synthesis: Rather than appropriating religious ideas without understanding, Larry engages deeply with the teachings and practices he encounters. He adapts them to his own spiritual journey, creating a personalized synthesis that reflects his quest for authenticity and meaning.

What about Appropriation? Is Larry a spiritual tourist? Or, is there something else at play?

Maybe the real question is: are we allowed to learn from the deep traditions and grand experiments of other cultures and apply some of their findings and practices to our own, dissimilar personal lives without being superficial, borrowing a teaching as if was a style, a fad or costume?

Defining Cultural Appropriation:

Cultural appropriation refers to the borrowing, adoption, or use of elements from one culture by members of another culture, often without understanding or respecting the original culture's significance or context. It can involve the appropriation of clothing, symbols, rituals, art, music, language, or other cultural elements. Cultural appropriation is a controversial issue when it is seen as disrespectful, insensitive, or reinforcing stereotypes. It is essential to engage in cross-cultural exchanges with sensitivity and respect for the origins and meanings of the borrowed elements.

1. Respectful Engagement: Larry approaches the religious and cultural traditions he encounters with respect and a genuine desire to learn. He does not engage in appropriation in a disrespectful or superficial way but rather seeks to understand and incorporate meaningful aspects into his own spiritual path.

2. Embracing Cultural Diversity: Larry's journey takes him to various parts of the world, where he engages with different cultures and traditions. He embraces the cultural diversity and learns from each context, avoiding cultural appropriation by respecting the integrity of each tradition.

3. Cultural Context: While Larry's spiritual journey is syncretic, it is also deeply rooted in the cultural and geographical contexts in which he finds himself. For example, his experiences in India and South-East Asia significantly shape his spiritual growth and understanding.

In essence, Larry's spiritual vision can be viewed as a form of religious syncretism, but it is marked by its personal and authentic nature. He is not appropriating religious thought for superficial reasons but is genuinely seeking to integrate meaningful insights from diverse traditions into his own spiritual evolution. His journey represents a quest for universal truths and a rejection of religious dogma in favor of a deeply personal and eclectic spiritual path.

Humility seems to be the key, here, seeking to engage in a cultural exchange with an open mind, a willingness to learn, and a commitment to respecting the source culture.

§

Larry Darrell - Intellectuals and Materialism

Larry's rejection of materialism is a central theme of the novel and is in direct contrast to characters like Elliott Templeton and Isabel Bradley, who prioritize social standing and material success.

Larry's journey represents a departure from the conventional values of the society he inhabits, and his rejection of materialism serves as a catalyst for his search for a more meaningful and authentic existence.

Several pre-World War I authors in the United States and, to a lesser extent, the United Kingdom and Europe, rejected materialism and explored themes related to spirituality, individualism, and non-conformity.

Here are a few notable authors who fit this description:

1. Henry David Thoreau (1817-1862):
Thoreau's works, particularly "Walden" and his essay "Civil Disobedience," emphasized the rejection of materialism and the value of simplicity and self-reliance. He advocated for a closer connection to nature and a minimalist lifestyle.

2. Ralph Waldo Emerson (1803-1882):
Emerson's essays, including "Self-Reliance" and "Nature," promoted individualism and self-reliance while critiquing societal conformity

and materialistic pursuits. His writings laid the foundation for the transcendentalist movement.

3. Walt Whitman (1819-1892):
Whitman's poetry, especially in "Leaves of Grass," celebrated the individual, the spiritual, and the connection between humanity and the natural world. He encouraged readers to find meaning beyond material possessions.

4. Leo Tolstoy (1828-1910):
Although Russian, Tolstoy's later works, such as "The Kingdom of God Is Within You," strongly rejected materialism and advocated for Christian pacifism, non-resistance to evil, and a simple, ascetic lifestyle.

5. George Bernard Shaw (1856-1950):
Shaw, an Irish playwright, used his plays, like "Man and Superman," to critique materialism and advocate for a more intellectual and spiritual approach to life, sometimes exploring themes related to Nietzschean individualism.

6. Oscar Wilde (1854-1900):
While Wilde is often associated with the Decadent movement, some of his works, such as "De Profundis," reflect his personal journey towards spiritual and moral self-discovery, which included a rejection of superficial materialism.

7. William James (1842-1910):
James, an American philosopher and psychologist, explored pragmatism and the concept of "radical empiricism," which challenged the materialistic reduction of human experience to scientific measurements.

These authors, while writing in different cultural and historical contexts, all engaged with themes of rejecting materialism, advocating for individualism, and exploring spirituality and non-conformity in their works. Their ideas contributed to the broader intellectual and philosophical discussions of their time and continue to resonate with readers today.

Characters in Depth - Isabel Bradley

Isabel Bradley is a character in W. Somerset Maugham's novel "The Razor's Edge." She is one of the central characters in the story, and her character reflects the influences and expectations of women of her time, which is the early 20th century.

Isabel is depicted as a young woman from a privileged background, and she represents the values and societal norms that were common for women of her social class during that era. Some of the influences and expectations that would have shaped her character as a woman of her time include:

1. Social Status and Marriage: Women of Isabel's social class were often expected to marry well and secure their social standing through advantageous marriages. Marriage was a primary concern for women, and they were often groomed for it from a young age.

2. Conventional Gender Roles: The early 20th century was a time when conventional gender roles were prevalent. Women were generally expected to be homemakers and mothers, with their primary role centered around the family and domestic life.

3. Societal Expectations: Society placed significant importance on a woman's reputation, conduct, and adherence to social conventions. Women were expected to conform to the expectations of polite society and maintain their social standing through proper behavior.

4. Limited Educational and Career Opportunities: Women of Isabel's background often had limited educational and career opportunities compared to men. Higher education and career aspirations were not as readily accessible to women as they are today.

5. Financial Dependency: Many women were financially dependent on their fathers or husbands. Financial independence was not as common for women of Isabel's social class during that time.

6. Marriage as a Life Goal: For women like Isabel, marriage was often seen as the ultimate life goal, and they were frequently pressured to marry for financial or social reasons rather than for love or personal fulfillment.

Throughout the novel, Isabel grapples with these societal expectations and values, particularly in her relationships with Larry Darrell and Gray Maturin. Her character's journey explores the tension between the societal pressures she faces as a woman of her time and her desires for personal happiness and fulfillment. Isabel's character serves as a reflection of the gender norms and social expectations prevalent during the early 20th century.

§

A contemporary reader of W. Somerset Maugham's novel "The Razor's Edge" might have several frustrations with the character of Isabel Bradley, as her actions and decisions can be seen through a modern lens as problematic or frustrating. Here are some potential frustrations:

1. Emphasis on Materialism: Isabel's strong emphasis on materialism, social status, and wealth can be frustrating to contemporary readers who value personal fulfillment, authenticity, and less materialistic pursuits.

2. Pressure to Conform: Isabel's tendency to conform to societal expectations and to prioritize societal norms over personal happiness can be frustrating to readers who champion individuality and the pursuit of one's own path.

3. Treatment of Larry: Isabel's treatment of Larry Darrell, particularly her inability to understand or support his quest for meaning and spiritual growth, may be frustrating to readers who value empathy and open-mindedness.

4. Interference in Others' Lives: Some readers may find Isabel's attempts to control the lives and choices of those around her, including her cousin Sophie and her fiancé Gray, to be frustrating and overbearing.

5. Unwillingness to Change: Isabel's resistance to personal growth and her persistence in adhering to traditional values, even when they lead to unhappiness, might be frustrating to readers who value adaptability and self-awareness.

6. Prioritizing Social Appearances: Isabel's strong concern for social appearances and her desire to maintain her status can be frustrating to readers who believe in the importance of genuine relationships and self-fulfillment over societal approval.

It's important to remember that Isabel's character is a product of her time and societal influences, and her actions and decisions reflect the values and norms of the early 20th century. While her character may be frustrating to contemporary readers, her role in the novel serves to highlight the contrast between traditional societal expectations and the pursuit of individual happiness and fulfillment.

§

There are some positive aspects to Isabel Bradley's character in W. Somerset Maugham's novel "The Razor's Edge" beyond being a cautionary tale. While she represents certain values and behaviors that the author critiques, her character also serves to illustrate the complexities of human relationships and the challenges individuals face when navigating societal expectations. Here are a few positive takeaways from her character:

1. Realism and Depth: Isabel's character adds depth and realism to the novel. Her struggles with her own desires, societal pressures, and her relationships with other characters reflect the complexities of human emotions and the conflicts people often face when trying to reconcile their own aspirations with external expectations.

2. Contrast with Other Characters: Isabel's character serves as a stark contrast to characters like Larry Darrell, who pursue unconventional paths to self-fulfillment. This contrast highlights the tension between conforming to societal norms and seeking individual happiness, inviting readers to reflect on their own values and choices.

3. Opportunity for Growth: Throughout the novel, Isabel's character has moments of self-reflection and inner conflict. These moments offer opportunities for growth and personal development, even if she does not fully embrace them. Her character's journey can encourage readers to consider the importance of self-awareness and the potential for change.

4. Empathy and Understanding: Readers may develop empathy and understanding for Isabel's character as they witness her struggles and conflicts. This empathy can extend to recognizing the societal pressures that individuals, especially women of her time, often faced in making life choices.

While Isabel Bradley's character is often seen as representing certain cautionary aspects of societal conformity and materialism, her presence in the novel contributes to its complexity and provides opportunities for reflection and discussion about the values and choices that shape individuals' lives.

§

Characters in Depth - Elliott Templeton

Elliott Templeton is a prominent character in W. Somerset Maugham's novel "The Razor's Edge." He is an American expatriate living in Paris and is known for his adherence to social conventions and his pursuit of high society. Elliott Templeton represents several key themes and ideas in the novel.

1. Social Conformity: Elliott Templeton embodies the idea of strict adherence to social conventions and the pursuit of social status. He is deeply concerned with maintaining his position within high society and is willing to compromise his principles and personal happiness to achieve this.

2. Traditional Values: Elliott is a traditionalist who values the formalities and traditions associated with the upper echelons of society. He represents the old guard of American expatriates in Paris, and his character serves as a contrast to the novel's more unconventional characters like Larry Darrell.

3. Struggle for Acceptance: Despite his adherence to societal norms, Elliott faces a continuous struggle for acceptance within the social elite. His efforts to fit in and maintain his social standing are a central part of his character arc.

4. Influence of Class and Status: Elliott's character highlights the influence of class and social status in early 20th-century society. His interactions with other characters, particularly Isabel Bradley, illustrate the significance placed on social rank and how it can shape one's choices and relationships.

5. Loneliness and Isolation: Despite his social success, Elliott is portrayed as somewhat lonely and isolated. He often longs for deeper connections and genuine friendships, which underscores the emptiness that can result from a relentless pursuit of social status.

6. Conflict with Larry Darrell: Elliott's character is in direct conflict with Larry Darrell, who rejects materialism and seeks spiritual enlightenment. Their interactions highlight the clash between traditional values and the pursuit of deeper meaning and authenticity.

In the novel, Elliott Templeton serves as a complex character who embodies the tensions between tradition and nonconformity, social conformity and individualism, and the pursuit of societal acceptance and personal fulfillment. His interactions with other characters illuminate these themes and contribute to the novel's exploration of the human search for meaning and happiness.

§

Elliott Templeton is primarily depicted as a character deeply dedicated to keeping up appearances and adhering to social conventions. He is known for his pursuit of high society, social status, and maintaining his position among the elite expatriate circles in Paris. These pursuits often overshadow any other interests or passions he may have had.

His character serves as a foil to other characters, particularly Larry Darrell, who reject conventional values and seek a more authentic and meaningful life. In this way, Elliott's one-dimensional portrayal highlights the clash between tradition and nonconformity and serves as a commentary on societal norms and their impact on individuals.

§

Characters in Depth - Sophie MacDonald

Sophie MacDonald is a significant character in W. Somerset Maugham's novel "The Razor's Edge." She represents several themes and aspects of the novel, as well as the generation to which she belongs.

1. Lost Generation: Sophie is a member of the "Lost Generation," a term used to describe the generation that came of age during or immediately following World War I. This generation is often characterized by disillusionment, trauma, and a sense of aimlessness resulting from the war's devastation.

2. Tragedy and Loss: Sophie's character embodies the profound tragedy and loss experienced by her generation due to the war. She loses her husband, Bob, in the war, which has a lasting impact on her emotional well-being and outlook on life.

3. Emotional Turmoil: Sophie grapples with emotional turmoil, including grief, guilt, and addiction. Her character represents the psychological scars that many individuals of her generation carried as a result of the war's trauma.

4. Struggle for Redemption: Sophie's journey in the novel involves a struggle for redemption and healing. Her character reflects the desire of many in her generation to find a sense of purpose and meaning in the aftermath of the war.

5. Quest for Happiness: Like other characters in the novel, Sophie seeks happiness and fulfillment. Her choices and relationships reflect the search for personal happiness and the challenges faced by her generation in attaining it.

6. Complexity of Relationships: Sophie's relationships with other characters, particularly Larry Darrell, Isabel Bradley, and Elliott Templeton, illustrate the complexities of human relationships and the impact of personal trauma on those connections.

7. Self-Destruction and Recovery: Sophie's character undergoes a cycle of self-destructive behavior and attempts at recovery, mirroring the struggles faced by many in her generation as they tried to cope with the war's aftermath.

Sophie MacDonald serves as a lens through which the novel explores the impact of war on individuals and the pursuit of happiness and redemption in the face of profound loss and emotional turmoil. Her character represents the challenges and complexities of her generation, making her a significant and multifaceted figure in the story.

§

Sophie MacDonald in "The Razor's Edge" by W. Somerset Maugham grapples with a form of post-traumatic stress disorder (PTSD) stemming from the loss of her husband in World War I and the subsequent loss of her child. Her character exhibits classic symptoms, including emotional turmoil, guilt, and self-destructive behavior, often masked by alcohol addiction.

Sophie's experiences mirror the psychological scars and challenges faced by many individuals of her generation who endured the trauma of war. Her character underscores the enduring impact of wartime trauma on mental health and the complexities of healing and recovery in the aftermath of profound loss and emotional suffering.

1. PTSD: During and following World War I, various terms were used to describe the psychological and emotional distress experienced by soldiers, including "shell shock," "war neuroses," and "combat fatigue."

These terms reflected the understanding at the time that exposure to the extreme stress and horrors of warfare could lead to mental health issues. Soldiers who exhibited symptoms such as anxiety, dissociation, and emotional distress were often diagnosed with these conditions.

Sophie's character mirrors the emotional toll of World War I. She loses her husband in the war, experiences trauma and emotional scars akin to soldiers, copes through addiction, and struggles with relationships, highlighting the post-war trauma and the quest for healing depicted in the novel.

2. Addiction: Sophie turns to alcohol as a coping mechanism to numb her emotional pain. Her addiction becomes a significant part of her life, contributing to her self-destructive behavior.

3. Self-Destructive Behavior: Sophie's grief and addiction lead her to engage in self-destructive behavior, including a tumultuous and unhealthy relationship with another character, Larry Darrell. Her actions reflect her struggle to cope with her losses.

4. Desire for Redemption: Despite her self-destructive tendencies, Sophie also harbors a deep desire for redemption and healing. She seeks a sense of purpose and meaning in her life, attempting to break free from the cycle of addiction and despair.

5. Complex Relationships: Sophie's relationships with other characters in the novel, such as Larry Darrell and Isabel Bradley, become complex and fraught with tension. These relationships reflect her internal conflicts and her attempts to find solace and love.

6. Spiritual Exploration: As the novel progresses, Sophie's character embarks on a journey of spiritual exploration and self-discovery. She seeks answers to life's deeper questions and grapples with her own sense of spirituality.

Overall, the death of her husband and child serves as a catalyst for Sophie's character transformation. She experiences both profound suffering and a yearning for redemption, and her journey is one of self-discovery, healing, and the quest for meaning and happiness in the face of tragedy and loss.

Luxembourg Gardens 1920s
The beautiful Luxembourg Gardens are mentioned as a location where characters stroll and relax.

In the 1920s and 1930s, the Luxembourg Gardens in Paris remained a haven of beauty and leisure. These lush and meticulously maintained gardens featured manicured lawns, vibrant flowerbeds, and the iconic Medici Fountain. The classical French design, characterized by symmetrical layouts and ornate statues, retained its timeless appeal. Parisians and visitors sought solace here, indulging in picnics, leisurely strolls, or moments of quiet reflection.

The gardens also served as a cultural hub, hosting open-air concerts, art exhibitions, and gatherings of intellectuals. Families flocked to the playgrounds, while the ponds, tree-lined pathways, and inviting benches provided an idyllic escape amidst the shifting political and cultural landscape of the time.

Week 4:
Themes of Self-Actualization

The Eastern Spiritual Journey

There are several common themes and philosophical concepts that connect many Eastern religions and spiritual traditions. While the specifics can vary widely among different traditions, there are overarching ideas that serve as unifying threads. Some of these universal themes include:

1. Reincarnation: Many Eastern religions, including Hinduism, Buddhism, and Jainism, believe in the cycle of birth, death, and rebirth (reincarnation). This cycle continues until one achieves spiritual liberation or enlightenment.

2. Karma: The concept of karma, which is the idea that one's actions have consequences, is prevalent in Eastern religions. Positive actions lead to positive outcomes, while negative actions result in negative consequences in future lives.

3. Dharma: Dharma refers to the moral and ethical duties and responsibilities that individuals have in their lives. Fulfilling one's dharma is seen as a path to spiritual growth and harmony.

4. Meditation and Mindfulness: Many Eastern traditions emphasize the practice of meditation and mindfulness as a means to attain higher states of consciousness, self-awareness, and inner peace.

5. Non-Attachment: The idea of non-attachment to material possessions and desires is a common theme. It is believed that attachment leads to suffering, and spiritual growth involves letting go of such attachments.

6. Unity and Interconnectedness: Eastern religions often stress the interconnectedness of all living beings and the universe. The concept of a universal consciousness or oneness is prevalent in many traditions.

7. Renunciation: Some Eastern religious paths involve renunciation of worldly pleasures and material pursuits in favor of a simpler, more spiritually focused life.

8. Compassion and Nonviolence: Compassion and nonviolence are highly regarded virtues in Eastern religions. The practice of ahimsa, or non-violence, is central to many of these traditions.

9. Seeking Enlightenment: The ultimate goal in many Eastern religions is the pursuit of enlightenment, liberation from the cycle of rebirth, and the realization of one's true nature.

10. Teacher-Disciple Relationship: Many Eastern traditions emphasize the importance of a close relationship between a spiritual teacher (guru) and a disciple (shishya) for guidance and spiritual growth.

While these themes are prevalent in many Eastern religions, it's essential to recognize that there is significant diversity within and between these traditions. Each tradition may interpret and prioritize these themes differently, and beliefs and practices can vary widely. Additionally, some Eastern religions may have unique concepts and teachings that set them apart from others.

Larry's Experiences in India and the Search for Meaning

"The Razor's Edge" by W. Somerset Maugham explores several themes that align with Eastern spiritual and philosophical concepts, and Larry Darrell, one of the central characters, adopts some of these themes into his worldview. He most certainly does not adopt them all, nor are all traditions represented.

1. Seeking Enlightenment: Larry's quest for a meaningful life and his search for answers lead him on a journey that reflects the Eastern theme of seeking enlightenment. He is driven to understand the deeper meaning of life and to find a sense of purpose beyond conventional societal expectations.

2. Meditation and Mindfulness: Larry engages in meditation and mindfulness practices, which are key elements of Eastern spirituality. These practices help him cultivate self-awareness and inner peace.

3. Non-Attachment: Larry embraces non-attachment to material possessions and status. He rejects the pursuit of wealth and chooses a simpler, more spiritually focused life, mirroring the Eastern concept that attachment leads to suffering.

4. Compassion and Nonviolence: Larry embodies the values of compassion and non-violence. He shows compassion and understanding toward others, even those who may not understand his unconventional path.

5. Teacher-Disciple Relationship: Larry seeks guidance from spiritual teachers and gurus, reflecting the importance of the teacher-disciple relationship in Eastern spirituality. He learns from various mentors along his journey.

6. Renunciation: Larry renounces a conventional life and the pursuit of material success, opting for a life of spiritual exploration and service to others.

While Larry adopts these themes into his worldview and lifestyle, it's important to note that "The Razor's Edge" is not a religious or explicitly spiritual novel. Rather, it explores the philosophical and existential questions that drive Larry's search for meaning and truth. Larry's journey incorporates elements of Eastern spirituality and philosophy, demonstrating how these themes can resonate with individuals seeking a deeper understanding of life and their place in the world.

§

What is Left Out

While the novel touches upon elements of Eastern spirituality, such as Hinduism and Buddhism, it does not delve deeply into the various Eastern religions and religious practices that exist. Some traditions that are not extensively explored in the novel include:

1. Islam: The novel does not specifically explore Islamic spirituality or practices, despite the presence of a diverse religious and cultural landscape in the world. Islam is not a prominent theme in the story.

2. Jainism: Jainism, a religion that originated in India and emphasizes non-violence, asceticism, and spiritual liberation, is not a major focus in the novel. The story primarily centers on characters who are more aligned with Hindu and Buddhist philosophies.

3. Sikhism: Sikhism, another religion with roots in India, is not discussed in detail in the novel. The novel's primary spiritual themes are related to Hinduism and Buddhism.

4. Tantra: While the novel does mention the concept of Tantra briefly, it does not delve deeply into the complexities of Tantric practices, rituals, or philosophy.

It's important to note that "The Razor's Edge" is not an exhaustive exploration of Eastern religions or spiritual practices. Instead, it provides a narrative that revolves around the personal spiritual journeys of its characters, with an emphasis on themes like seeking meaning, enlightenment, and the rejection of materialism.

The story is not intended to be a comprehensive study of Eastern religions but rather a work of fiction that incorporates elements of spirituality and philosophical exploration.

§

That being said, there are some majour omissions even in the passages about Hinduism and Buddhism, that neglect to address the full breadth and complexity of these religions. Some aspects of Hinduism and Buddhism that are not extensively explored in the novel include:

1. Hindu Deities: The novel does not delve into the rich pantheon of Hindu deities or their associated myths and stories. It focuses more on the philosophical and spiritual aspects of Hinduism.

2. Hindu Rituals: While the novel briefly mentions rituals and ceremonies, it does not provide an in-depth exploration of Hindu rituals, including worship practices, festivals, and religious rites.

3. Hindu Caste System: The novel does not extensively discuss the Hindu caste system, which is a significant social and cultural aspect of Hinduism.

4. Buddhist Schools: Buddhism encompasses various schools and traditions, each with its own interpretations and practices. The novel primarily touches upon Buddhist concepts related to suffering and enlightenment without delving into the distinctions between different Buddhist schools.

5. Meditation Techniques: While the characters in the novel engage in meditation and spiritual introspection, the specific meditation techniques associated with Hinduism and Buddhism are not described in great detail.

6. Yoga: Yoga, a significant practice in both Hinduism and Buddhism, is briefly mentioned in the novel, but the various forms and branches of yoga are not explored comprehensively.

7. Sacred Texts: The novel does not delve into the sacred texts and scriptures of Hinduism and Buddhism, such as the Vedas, Upanishads, Bhagavad Gita, or Buddhist sutras.

8. Monastic Life: While there are characters in the novel who pursue spiritual paths, the novel does not provide an extensive look into the life of Hindu or Buddhist monks and monastic communities.

Maugham chooses to use elements of Hinduism and Buddhism as a backdrop for exploring existential and philosophical themes. The focus is on the personal spiritual journeys of the characters rather than providing a comprehensive or scholarly examination of these religions. Future stories using different aspects of the same religions might turn out far different that the novel we are focusing on at the moment.

§

Not that I would have much patience for it, and knowing there is certainly no place for it in this novel, I am intrigued by the traditions of the "holy fool" or "divine madman" in some Eastern religions and spiritual traditions of India, particularly within Hinduism and certain sects of Bhakti and Tantra.

The concept of the holy fool is associated with individuals who exhibit eccentric or unconventional behavior as a means of expressing their deep spirituality and connection to the divine. Perhaps this is what Bill Murray was trying to tap into in his film version of "The Razor's Edge"?

Some key points related to the holy fool tradition in India include:

1. Bhakti and Sant Traditions: Within Hinduism, the Bhakti movement and the Sant traditions (associated with saint-poets like Kabir, Ravidas, and Tukaram) have featured holy fools. These individuals may engage in seemingly irrational acts, such as dancing, singing, or behaving in socially unconventional ways, to convey their intense devotion and divine ecstasy.

2. Outward Eccentricity: Holy fools often appear eccentric or even mad in their outward behavior. They may disregard societal norms, dress in unusual clothing, or engage in spontaneous and unscripted acts that challenge conventional expectations.

3. Divine Inspiration: Holy fools claim to be inspired and guided by a higher spiritual truth or a direct connection to the divine. Their actions are seen as a reflection of their deep inner realization and spiritual ecstasy.

4. Teaching Through Paradox: The holy fool tradition often employs paradox and irony to convey profound spiritual teachings. By defying conventional wisdom and expectations, these individuals encourage followers to look beyond surface appearances and delve into deeper spiritual truths.

5. Cultural Variation: The holy fool tradition can vary among different regions and sects in India. Some holy fools may be revered as saints and spiritual guides, while others are seen as unconventional wanderers.

6. Cultural Influences: The concept of the holy fool in India may have been influenced by similar traditions in other parts of the world, such as the concept of the "fool for Christ" in Eastern Orthodox Christianity.

Overall, the holy fool tradition in India reflects the diversity and richness of spiritual expression within Hinduism and related traditions. These individuals challenge societal norms and invite seekers to explore the boundaries of conventional wisdom in their quest for spiritual understanding and divine connection.

§

Hindu Temple, India 1920s

Crafted over generations, these architectural marvels bear witness to centuries of devotion. The intricate designs and ornate carvings, taking decades or even centuries to build, are a testament to the unwavering dedication of countless artisans and devotees who shaped these sacred edifices.

Buddhist Temple, India 1920s

In the serene ambiance of 1920s India, a Buddhist temple stands as a tranquil oasis of spiritual contemplation. Its elegant architecture, adorned with intricate carvings and delicate artistry, reflects the profound grace of Buddhist devotion. Time, measured not in years but in generations, was invested in the temple's creation—a labor of love by skilled artisans who meticulously sculpted each stone. As the sun casts gentle shadows on this sacred sanctuary, it embodies the essence of Buddhism's timeless wisdom and the quiet resilience of a faith that has endured for centuries.

Week 5:
Themes of Self-Delusion

Materialism and Societal Pressures

Post-World War I society experienced significant tensions related to materialism and societal pressures. The war itself had a profound impact on people's perceptions and priorities, contributing to these tensions in several ways:

1. Materialism and Consumerism: The aftermath of World War I brought about a surge in materialism and consumerism. Many returning soldiers and civilians were eager to enjoy the comforts and luxuries they had been deprived of during the war. There was a strong desire for consumer goods, leading to economic prosperity but also fostering a culture of material excess.

2. The Lost Generation: A term coined by writer Gertrude Stein, the "Lost Generation" referred to the disillusioned and spiritually adrift individuals who came of age during or after World War I. These young adults, having witnessed the horrors of war, felt disconnected from traditional values and societal norms. Their disillusionment often led to a search for meaning beyond material pursuits.

3. Societal Pressures: Post-war society placed immense pressure on individuals to conform to conventional expectations, including pursuing careers, marriage, and raising families. The pressure to conform to societal norms could be stifling, leading many to question whether these pursuits truly brought fulfillment.

4. Existential Crisis: The war's brutality and the loss of millions of lives prompted deep existential questions about the meaning of life and the nature of humanity. Many people grappled with profound existential crises, seeking answers beyond material success.

5. Spiritual and Philosophical Exploration: In response to the materialism and conformity of the post-war period, some individuals turned to spiritual and philosophical exploration. They sought solace and purpose in Eastern philosophies, mysticism, and non-traditional belief systems, as depicted in "The Razor's Edge" and other works of literature from the time.

6. Cultural and Artistic Movements: The tensions surrounding materialism and societal pressures influenced cultural and artistic movements, such as the Roaring Twenties in the United States and the Dadaist and Surrealist movements in Europe. These movements often critiqued the shallowness of materialistic values.

Overall, the post-World War I era was marked by a complex interplay between the pursuit of material success and the search for deeper meaning. The tensions arising from these contrasting forces shaped the cultural and intellectual landscape of the time, fostering both material excess and a quest for spiritual and philosophical fulfillment.

§

The post-World War I tensions related to materialism and societal pressures can indeed be connected to a sense of loss of self, particularly in the context of a multi-dimensional self with community ties and diverse skills and interests. Here's how:

1. Fragmentation of Identity: The war's traumas and the subsequent societal emphasis on material success often fragmented individuals' identities. Many people felt torn between the demands of societal conformity and their desire to retain or rediscover their multi-dimensional selves. This fragmentation contributed to a sense of loss and inner conflict.

2. Loss of Community Ties: The war disrupted communities and social bonds as people were uprooted from their homes and communities to serve in the conflict. After the war, returning veterans and civilians alike found that the communities they once belonged to had changed or disappeared altogether. This loss of community ties could leave individuals feeling isolated and disconnected from their support networks.

3. Pressure to Conform: The societal pressures to conform to traditional roles and expectations, such as pursuing a career and starting a family, often led individuals to suppress or neglect their diverse skills and interests. The pressure to conform could result in a narrowing of one's identity, as people focused on meeting external expectations rather than pursuing their passions.

4. Search for Authenticity: In response to these pressures and the sense of loss, some individuals embarked on journeys of self-discovery and a quest for authenticity. They sought to reconnect with their multi-dimensional selves, exploring their diverse interests and talents, and often rejecting the shallow materialism of the time.

5. Spiritual and Philosophical Exploration: Many individuals turned to spiritual and philosophical pursuits as a means of finding a deeper sense of self and purpose. These explorations often involved a rejection of materialism in favor of a more holistic and meaningful way of life.

In literature and cultural narratives of the era, characters like Larry Darrell in "The Razor's Edge" represent individuals who grapple with these complex issues. They seek to reclaim a sense of self that encompasses a range of skills, interests, and a deeper connection to their own authenticity.

The tension between societal pressures and the desire for a more profound and multi-dimensional self is a recurring theme in post-World War I literature and reflects the broader societal shifts and challenges of the time.

§

The Disillusionment of Isabel and Elliott

In W. Somerset Maugham's novel "The Razor's Edge," both Elliot Templeton and Isabel Bradshaw are portrayed as characters who experience a form of disillusionment and engage in self-deception to navigate their lives.

1. Elliot Templeton: Elliot is a socialite and expatriate who is deeply embedded in the upper echelons of European society. He is disillusioned in the sense that he places immense importance on social status, appearance, and maintaining an image of refinement and cultural superiority. Despite his wealth and social connections, he is often depicted as shallow and superficial. Elliot engages in self-deception by prioritizing appearances over substance, clinging to an elitist worldview, and ignoring the emptiness that lies beneath his glamorous facade. He lies to himself by pretending that his social standing and connections define his worth, even as he sees those around him pursue more meaningful paths.

2. Isabel Bradshaw: Isabel is initially depicted as a young woman who values material comfort and societal expectations. She becomes disillusioned when she realizes that her marriage to Larry Darrell, a character who seeks spiritual and philosophical enlightenment, does not align with her own materialistic desires. She engages in self-deception by convincing herself that her pursuit of wealth and social standing is the path to happiness. She lies to herself by ignoring her true feelings and desires, ultimately leading to an unsatisfying and unfulfilling life.

Both Elliot and Isabel represent characters who are trapped in a cycle of societal expectations and materialism, which leads to their disillusionment. They engage in self-deception as a coping mechanism to maintain their chosen lifestyles and avoid confronting the emptiness or unhappiness that lies beneath the surface. Their journeys highlight the theme of the pursuit of authenticity and meaning in a world that often prioritizes superficiality and conformity.

§

Sophie's Struggle with Addiction

Sophie MacDonald, a character in W. Somerset Maugham's novel "The Razor's Edge," undergoes a complex and tragic journey marked by struggles with addiction and self-deception. Her story illustrates the destructive consequences of trying to fit into societal norms and later descending into the depths of addiction.

1. Early Self-Deception and Attempt to Conform: Sophie initially tries to conform to societal expectations and the bourgeois lifestyle. She marries a wealthy man, and for a time, she embraces the trappings of wealth and social status. However, she quickly becomes disillusioned with this lifestyle, realizing that materialism and conformity do not bring her true happiness. This initial self-deception involves her attempt to fit into a prescribed societal mold that doesn't align with her inner desires.

2. Descent into Addiction: As Sophie's marriage unravels, she turns to alcohol as a form of escapism. Her addiction to alcohol deepens over time, and she eventually becomes entangled in a self-destructive cycle of drinking and self-harming behavior. Her addiction serves as a means of numbing emotional pain and suppressing the inner turmoil she feels.

3. Self-Deception and Denial: Sophie engages in self-deception as she denies the severity of her addiction and its detrimental effects on her life. She often rationalizes her behavior, believing that she can control her drinking or that it provides her with a temporary respite from her troubles. This denial allows her to continue down a path of self-destruction.

4. Loss of Self: Sophie's addiction ultimately leads to a loss of self. She becomes increasingly disconnected from her true identity and the person she once was. Her addiction defines her existence, overshadowing her previous aspirations and potential for a meaningful life.

5. Seeking Redemption: Sophie's story is one of tragedy and redemption. She reaches a point where she acknowledges the depth of her addiction and the harm it has caused. Her journey toward recovery and redemption becomes a central theme in the latter part of the novel.

Sophie's struggle with addiction and self-deception serves as a poignant exploration of the human capacity for self-destructive behavior and the desire for redemption. Her character highlights the importance of confronting one's demons and seeking help when caught in a cycle of addiction and denial. In the context of the novel, her journey is a reflection of the broader theme of individuals' quests for meaning and authenticity in the face of societal pressures and personal struggles.

Week 6:
Love and Relationships

Larry and Isabel: Love and Loss

In W. Somerset Maugham's novel "The Razor's Edge," Isabel Bradshaw loses Larry Darrell for several reasons:

1. Different Life Paths: Larry and Isabel have fundamentally different life paths and priorities. After World War I, Larry undergoes a profound transformation and seeks spiritual enlightenment and meaning in life. His quest leads him to travel and pursue a simpler, more contemplative existence. Isabel, on the other hand, values material success, social standing, and conformity to societal norms. Their contrasting aspirations and values make it challenging for them to reconcile their differences.

2. Incompatibility: As Larry's spiritual and philosophical interests deepen, he realizes that he and Isabel are fundamentally incompatible. He values inner growth and authenticity, while Isabel is primarily focused on external appearances and societal expectations. This incompatibility leads to a growing emotional distance between them.

3. Larry's Rejection: Larry ultimately rejects Isabel's proposal of marriage because he understands that their paths have diverged too significantly. He refuses to enter into a marriage that he knows would be based on compromise and a denial of his true self.

Isabel's decision to marry Gray Maturin is driven by her desire for financial security and societal acceptance. Gray offers her stability and the comforts of wealth, which align with her materialistic aspirations. It's implied that she marries Gray because she believes he can provide the kind of life she desires.

It's unlikely that Larry would have married Isabel even if she had waited. Larry's transformation and spiritual quest are central to his character, and he is unwavering in his commitment to seeking meaning beyond materialism and societal expectations. He recognizes that he and Isabel are on divergent paths and that a marriage between them would not be fulfilling for either party. Larry's journey is a search for authenticity and a rejection of superficiality, which makes it improbable that he would have chosen a conventional marriage with Isabel even if she had been patient.

Sophie and Larry: Compassion and Codependency

W. Somerset Maugham's novel "The Razor's Edge," the relationship between Sophie MacDonald and Larry Darrell is a complex and compelling exploration of compassion, codependency, and the boundless nature of Larry's compassion. Here's an analysis:

1. Compassion for Sophie: Larry Darrell's compassion for Sophie MacDonald is a central theme in the novel. Sophie, a troubled and self-destructive character, is initially married to Larry's close friend, Gray Maturin. When Sophie's life takes a tragic turn due to her addiction and personal struggles, Larry shows deep empathy and concern for her well-being. His compassion for her reflects his underlying belief in the value of every individual, regardless of their flaws.

2. Codependency: Sophie's character struggles with addiction and self-destructive behavior, and she becomes emotionally dependent on Larry for support and stability. On the other hand, Larry feels a strong sense of responsibility for Sophie's welfare due to his compassion. This dynamic borders on codependency, as both characters rely on each other to fulfill emotional needs. Larry's compassion for Sophie often leads him to make sacrifices for her, both emotionally and materially.

3. Boundless Nature of Larry's Compassion: Larry's compassion is portrayed as boundless and unconditional. He is willing to help and support Sophie even when it seems futile or when others have given up on her. This boundless compassion reflects Larry's broader spiritual journey, where he seeks to embody love, understanding, and empathy toward all beings.

4. Personal Sacrifice: Larry's compassion for Sophie comes at a personal cost. He devotes significant time, energy, and resources to help her, even when it means postponing his own spiritual pursuits. His willingness to make such sacrifices underscores the depth of his compassion and his commitment to helping those in need.

5. Impact on Larry: Larry's boundless compassion for Sophie takes a toll on him, both emotionally and spiritually. He grapples with the challenges of supporting someone battling addiction and self-destructive tendencies. While his compassion is genuine, it also becomes a test of his own spiritual strength and resilience.

In the novel, Larry's compassion for Sophie serves as a microcosm of his larger spiritual journey. It illustrates his commitment to embodying compassion and understanding in a world often characterized by materialism and superficiality. Their relationship highlights the complexities of compassion, including its potential to lead to codependency and personal sacrifice.

Ultimately, Larry's boundless compassion for Sophie underscores his quest for authenticity and his belief in the transformative power of love and understanding.

§

The Role of Relationships in Self-Discovery

In "The Razor's Edge" by W. Somerset Maugham, relationships play a significant role in the process of self-discovery for the novel's characters. Each character's journey of self-discovery is influenced by their interactions with others, and these relationships serve as catalysts for personal growth and transformation. Here's an exploration of the role of relationships in self-discovery in the novel:

1. Larry and Isabel: The relationship between Larry Darrell and Isabel Bradshaw is central to the novel. It highlights the tension between pursuing one's individual quest for meaning and conforming to societal expectations. Larry's rejection of Isabel's materialistic and conventional values prompts his spiritual journey, while Isabel's inability to understand Larry's quest forces her to confront her own shallowness and unexamined beliefs.

2. Larry and Sophie: Larry's relationship with Sophie MacDonald demonstrates his capacity for compassion and empathy. Sophie's struggles with addiction and self-destructive behavior become a testing ground for Larry's commitment to unconditional love and understanding. This relationship challenges Larry's spiritual ideals and his ability to help others in their own paths of self-discovery.

3. Elliott Templeton: Elliott Templeton, a superficial and elitist character, represents the antithesis of Larry's values. His relationships within the high-society expatriate community expose the emptiness of his own existence and highlight the contrast between materialism and spiritual fulfillment.

4. Isabel and Gray: Isabel's marriage to Gray Maturin underscores her commitment to conventional values and her fear of deviating from societal norms. Her interactions with Gray reveal her struggle to find contentment within a traditional marriage, ultimately leading her to question her own choices and priorities.

5. Maugham as the Narrator: The relationship between the author, W. Somerset Maugham, and the characters is unique. Maugham, who serves as the novel's narrator, interacts with the characters and observes their journeys. His role as an observer and participant in their lives allows him to reflect on their experiences, providing insights into their paths of self-discovery.

In "The Razor's Edge," relationships serve as mirrors, reflecting the characters' inner conflicts, values, and desires. Through their interactions with one another, the characters confront societal norms, materialism, and existential questions. These relationships challenge them to examine their own beliefs and priorities, ultimately leading to varying degrees of self-discovery and personal transformation. The novel underscores the idea that meaningful relationships can be catalysts for individuals to embark on profound journeys of self-exploration and authenticity.

§

Personal Relationships in America between WW1 and The Great Depression

Between World War I and the Great Depression, the dynamics of personal and community relationships in America underwent significant changes, reflecting the broader societal shifts and challenges of the era. Here's an exploration of these changes and how people relied on personal connections for self-improvement:

1. Personal Relationships:

Changing Gender Roles: The aftermath of World War I saw shifting gender roles as women gained more independence and entered the workforce during the war. This change affected personal relationships as traditional family dynamics evolved.

Individualism and Self-Exploration: The period between the wars witnessed a growing emphasis on individualism and self-exploration. Personal relationships, particularly romantic ones, often became a platform for individuals to seek meaning, authenticity, and compatibility.

2. Community Relationships:

Urbanization: The 1920s brought about increased urbanization, with people moving to cities for economic opportunities. This shift disrupted traditional community structures, as individuals became more disconnected from their rural roots and extended families.

Cultural Movements: The era saw the rise of cultural movements like the Harlem Renaissance and the Jazz Age, which fostered new forms of community and artistic expression. These movements offered opportunities for connection and self-expression beyond traditional community boundaries.

3. Reliance on Personal Connections for Self-Improvement:

Social Support Networks: During the economic challenges of the Great Depression, personal relationships became crucial for social support. Families, friends, and close-knit communities often relied on one another for emotional and financial assistance.

Mentorship and Guidance: Personal relationships, including mentorship, played a role in helping individuals navigate the changing economic landscape. Mentors could provide guidance and support in career development and self-improvement.

Crisis Response: In the face of economic hardship, personal connections were essential for collective responses. Communities organized relief efforts, mutual aid societies, and volunteer initiatives to support those in need.

Overall, the period between World War I and the Great Depression marked a transition in personal and community relationships. While personal relationships increasingly became a means of self-expression and self-discovery, community relationships evolved in response to urbanization and cultural shifts. The economic challenges of the Great Depression reinforced the importance of personal connections for support and mutual assistance, highlighting the resilience of individuals and communities during difficult times. Personal relationships continued to serve as a vital resource for self-improvement and collective well-being in an evolving American society.

§

Community Church, NYC, 1930s

During the Great Depression in New York City, churches played a
vital role in providing assistance to those in need. They established
soup kitchens, shelters, and community programs, offering not only
material support but also a sense of hope and solidarity in the face of
economic hardship.

Week 7:
Ethics and Self-Deception

Larry's Ethical Dilemmas

Larry Darrell, the protagonist of W. Somerset Maugham's novel "The Razor's Edge," faces several ethical dilemmas throughout the story. His character undergoes a transformation as he seeks meaning and purpose in life, and his Eastern learning plays a significant role in how he approaches and resolves these conflicts. Here are some of the ethical dilemmas Larry faces and how he applies his Eastern teachings to address them:

1. Materialism vs. Spiritual Fulfillment: Larry initially grapples with the materialistic values of his society, particularly the pursuit of wealth and social status. He inherits a considerable fortune but chooses to reject a conventional life in favor of seeking spiritual fulfillment. Larry's exposure to Eastern philosophies, particularly Vedanta and Buddhism, encourages him to prioritize inner peace and self-realization over material possessions. He applies the principle of detachment, which he learns from these philosophies, to free himself from the trappings of materialism.

2. Love and Relationships: Larry's romantic relationships present ethical dilemmas, especially his engagement to Isabel and his deep connection with Sophie. He struggles with the expectations placed on him by society and the conflicts arising from his evolving spiritual values. Eastern teachings emphasize compassion and empathy, and Larry applies these principles in his relationships by offering support and understanding to Sophie, who faces personal challenges, without judgment or condemnation.

3. Responsibility to Others: Larry's decision to pursue a spiritual path raises questions about his responsibilities to his family and loved ones. His aunt, Mrs. Bradley, is concerned about his choices and the impact they might have on her family's reputation. Larry seeks a balance between fulfilling his own spiritual quest and fulfilling his responsibilities, which aligns with the Eastern concept of dharma (duty) and karma (the consequences of one's actions). He strives to act in ways that are in harmony with his own inner truth and moral values while minimizing harm to others.

4. War and Violence: Larry's experiences in World War I expose him to the horrors of violence and death. This traumatic experience raises ethical questions about the nature of war and humanity's capacity for violence. Larry's Eastern learning teaches him non-violence (ahimsa) and the importance of inner peace. He grapples with these lessons as he seeks to reconcile the violence he witnessed with his newfound spiritual ideals.

Larry Darrell's journey in "The Razor's Edge" is a quest for self-discovery and ethical clarity. His Eastern teachings provide him with tools and perspectives that help him navigate these ethical dilemmas. Through meditation, introspection, and a commitment to inner growth, he seeks to align his actions with his deeper understanding of life's purpose and meaning, ultimately choosing a path that reflects his commitment to spiritual fulfillment and ethical living.

§

The Consequences of Deception in the Novel

In W. Somerset Maugham's novel "The Razor's Edge," the consequences of characters deceiving themselves and others play a significant role in the development of the story and its themes. Here are some key consequences of deception in the novel:

1. Unfulfilled Lives: One of the central themes of the novel is the pursuit of meaning and purpose in life. Characters like Isabel and her uncle Elliott often deceive themselves by clinging to superficial values and societal expectations. They lead lives that, from the outside, may seem successful but lack true fulfillment. Their deception about what constitutes a meaningful life ultimately leaves them unfulfilled.

2. Strained Relationships: Deception and self-deception strain relationships in the novel. Isabel's desire to marry Larry Darrell, despite her concerns about his spiritual quest, creates tension between them. Larry's honesty about his priorities ultimately leads to the end of their engagement. Likewise, the strained relationship between Larry and Isabel's uncle, Elliott, is a result of their conflicting values and beliefs.

3. Loss of Authenticity: Characters who engage in self-deception lose touch with their authentic selves. They become disconnected from their true desires and values, often pursuing material success or social status at the expense of their own authenticity. This loss of authenticity can lead to feelings of emptiness and dissatisfaction.

4. Missed Opportunities: Self-deception can lead characters to miss out on opportunities for personal growth and enlightenment. Larry Darrell's rejection of materialism and pursuit of a more meaningful life is a response to the realization that he could not live inauthentically or compromise his beliefs. Other characters who deceive themselves miss the chance for similar personal growth and self-discovery.

5. Irony and Critique: Maugham uses the consequences of deception to provide a critique of societal values and expectations. He employs irony to contrast the lives of characters like Larry, who seek authenticity and meaning, with those who deceive themselves and conform to societal norms. The novel highlights the irony that some characters lead seemingly successful lives but are spiritually impoverished, while others who reject conventionality find deeper meaning.

In "The Razor's Edge," the consequences of deception serve to underscore the novel's exploration of themes related to the search for meaning, authenticity, and the clash between materialism and spirituality. Characters' choices to deceive themselves or others have far-reaching effects on their lives and relationships, ultimately driving the narrative and conveying Maugham's commentary on the human condition.

§

Philosophical Perspectives on Truth and Honesty

Philosophical perspectives on truth and honesty have been explored across various cultures and time periods, including the United States (U.S.), the United Kingdom (U.K.), France, India, and Japan. Here's a brief overview of these perspectives from antiquity to the 1940s in each of these regions:

1. Antiquity:

Greece: In ancient Greece, philosophers like Socrates, Plato, and Aristotle laid the foundation for discussions on truth and honesty. Socrates emphasized the pursuit of truth through questioning and self-examination, while Plato explored concepts of truth in his dialogues. Aristotle, in his Nicomachean Ethics, discussed the virtue of honesty and its role in moral character.

2. United States and United Kingdom:

17th-18th Century: Philosophers like John Locke and Thomas Hobbes in the U.K. and John Stuart Mill and Ralph Waldo Emerson in the U.S. discussed concepts related to truth and honesty. Locke's empiricism influenced ideas about the correspondence theory of truth, where truth is the agreement between belief and reality.

19th-20th Century: Pragmatism emerged in the U.S., with thinkers like Charles Peirce and William James. Pragmatism views truth as a function of usefulness and practical consequences. In the U.K., philosophers like G.E. Moore discussed the nature of truth and defended common-sense realism.

3. France:

17th-18th Century: René Descartes is a notable French philosopher who contributed to discussions on truth. His famous statement "Cogito, ergo sum" ("I think, therefore I am") is foundational in epistemology and truth theory.

20th Century: Existentialist philosophers like Jean-Paul Sartre explored the idea of personal authenticity and honesty with oneself, emphasizing individual responsibility for defining one's truth.

4. India:

Ancient Period: Indian philosophy, particularly within schools like Nyaya and Vedanta, delved into the nature of truth and reality. The concept of "Satyam" (truth) is a fundamental principle in Indian thought.

20th Century: Figures like Mahatma Gandhi emphasized truth (Satya) and non-violence (Ahimsa) as core principles in the pursuit of justice and social change.

5. Japan:

Ancient and Medieval Periods: Japanese philosophy, influenced by Buddhism and Confucianism, often emphasized moral and ethical dimensions of truth and honesty. Honesty in interpersonal relationships was highly regarded.

20th Century: Japanese philosophers like Kitaro Nishida engaged in discussions on existentialism and the nature of self, exploring truth and authenticity in an evolving cultural context.

Throughout these regions and time periods, philosophical perspectives on truth and honesty have evolved, incorporating cultural, historical, and individual contexts. These perspectives continue to influence contemporary discussions on ethics, epistemology, and the human condition.

§

Nothing Like the Truth: Power and Deception

Be prepared, Dear Reader. Not everyone tells the truth. In Modern life, Gurus and pick-up artists can employ various tactics in their interactions with people, and some individuals within these groups may resort to deception or manipulation to achieve their goals. However, it's important to note that not all gurus or pick-up artists engage in deceptive practices, and there is a wide range of approaches within these communities.

1. Gurus:

Gurus, spiritual leaders, or self-help figures may genuinely aim to provide guidance and support to their followers. They often share their insights and knowledge to help individuals improve their lives and achieve personal growth.

However, there have been instances of fraudulent gurus who use deception to exploit their followers, including financial scams, false claims of spiritual attainment, and manipulation of vulnerable individuals. These deceptive practices can have harmful consequences for those who trust and follow them.

2. Pick-Up Artists (PUAs):

Pick-up artists are individuals who often focus on improving their dating and social skills, primarily with the goal of initiating romantic or sexual relationships.

Some PUAs may employ manipulative techniques and deceptive tactics to try to attract romantic partners. These tactics can include negging (insulting or undermining someone to lower their self-esteem), using scripted lines, or attempting to manipulate emotions.

 It's important to note that many people within the PUA community and the broader self-improvement community advocate for ethical and respectful approaches to dating and relationships, emphasizing consent, communication, and genuine connection.

In both cases, it's crucial for individuals to exercise caution and critical thinking when encountering gurus or pick-up artists. People should be aware of the potential for deception and manipulation and make informed decisions about the advice and guidance they choose to follow. Healthy relationships, whether they involve personal growth or dating, are typically built on honesty, respect, and genuine connections rather than deceptive tactics.

§

Believing a Pick-Up Artist (PUA) or a guru with bad intentions can be an example of self-deception for several reasons.

1. Desire for Personal Improvement: People who seek out PUAs or gurus often do so with the genuine desire to improve themselves, whether in the realm of dating and relationships or personal development. This desire for self-improvement can lead individuals to overlook or rationalize red flags and deceptive tactics employed by these figures.

2. Confirmation Bias: Self-deception often involves selective attention to information that confirms one's existing beliefs or desires. People may ignore warning signs or evidence of a PUA or guru's manipulative behavior because they are so invested in the idea that following their guidance will lead to personal growth or success.

3. Vulnerability and Emotional Investment: Individuals who turn to PUAs or gurus are often in vulnerable emotional states, seeking guidance or validation. They may be more susceptible to manipulation due to their emotional needs, and they may deceive themselves by convincing themselves that the PUA or guru genuinely cares about their well-being.

4. Cognitive Dissonance: When someone invests time, money, and emotional energy in following a PUA or guru, they may experience cognitive dissonance if they start to see signs of deception or manipulation. To resolve this dissonance, they might engage in self-deception by downplaying or rationalizing these negative aspects.

5. Social Proof and Groupthink: Belonging to a community or group that follows a PUA or guru can create social pressure to conform to the group's beliefs and values. This can lead individuals to deceive themselves into accepting the group's perspective, even if it goes against their better judgment.

6. Hope and Optimism: Self-deception can also stem from a deep sense of hope and optimism. People may want to believe that the PUA or guru is a genuine source of wisdom or guidance, and they may deceive themselves into thinking that the negative aspects are mere exceptions or misunderstandings.

Ultimately, self-deception in these situations often involves a complex interplay of psychological factors, including cognitive biases, emotional vulnerabilities, and social influences. People may genuinely want to believe that they are making positive changes in their lives, which can lead them to overlook or rationalize the negative aspects of following a PUA or guru with bad intentions. Recognizing self-deception and critically evaluating the credibility and intentions of such figures can be a challenging but essential process for individuals seeking genuine personal growth and well-being.

§

During the early 20th century, there were several individuals who posed as spiritual leaders or gurus and gained followings, but their intentions were questioned, and they were later revealed to be false. Here are three examples from that era:

1. Jiddu Krishnamurti's Early Spiritual Leader (1909-1929): Jiddu Krishnamurti was a young boy from India who was groomed to be the World Teacher by the Theosophical Society. He was promoted as a messianic figure, but in 1929, he dissolved the Order of the Star, the organization built around him, and renounced his role as a spiritual leader. Krishnamurti spent the rest of his life advocating for personal inquiry and rejecting guru-like status.

2. "The Great Oom" (Pierre Bernard, 1920s): Pierre Bernard, known as "The Great Oom," was an American yogi who gained fame for his yoga teachings in the 1920s. While he had some genuine knowledge of yoga and meditation, he was also accused of financial improprieties and sexual misconduct. His reputation suffered, and his yoga community disbanded.

3. "Brother Twelve" (Edward Arthur Wilson, 1920s): Edward Arthur Wilson, a Canadian mystic who went by the name "Brother Twelve," founded a spiritual commune on Vancouver Island. He claimed to be a prophet and gained a following, but his leadership was marred by allegations of fraud, manipulation, and unethical behavior. His commune eventually dissolved amid controversy.

These examples illustrate how charismatic figures can attract followers by presenting themselves as spiritual leaders, only to later reveal ulterior motives or engage in unethical behavior. The early 20th century saw a proliferation of such figures, and their stories highlight the importance of critical discernment and skepticism when evaluating spiritual leaders and gurus.

The Ganges River, 1925

In 1925, the Ganges River held immense importance in India's cultural milieu. It was regarded as holy and purifying in Hinduism, and millions of pilgrims flocked to its banks to cleanse themselves of sins through ritual baths. The river was also a lifeline, sustaining communities along its course. However, even then, signs of environmental degradation were evident. The cultural reverence for the Ganges coexisted with growing pollution concerns, primarily from industrial effluents and human waste. The juxtaposition of holiness and pollution around the Ganges foreshadowed later challenges in maintaining its purity and underscores the ongoing struggle to balance cultural significance with environmental preservation.

Week 8:
Contemporary Perspectives

Modern Interpretations of Self-Actualization

The concept of self-actualization and personal growth has evolved over the 20th and 21st centuries, with various paradigms emerging in response to changing societal, cultural, and psychological factors. Here is an overview of modern paradigms for self-actualization from the 1920s to the present day:

1. 1920s-1930s: Humanistic Psychology and Self-Exploration
This era saw the emergence of humanistic psychology, with figures like Abraham Maslow and Carl Rogers advocating for the importance of self-actualization as the highest level of psychological development.

Self-actualization was associated with fulfilling one's potential, pursuing authentic goals, and embracing personal growth through self-exploration and self-acceptance.

2. 1960s-1970s: The Me-Generation and Counterculture
The 1960s and 1970s witnessed the rise of the "Me-Generation," characterized by a focus on self-expression, individualism, and personal liberation.

The counterculture movement emphasized self-discovery through experiences like psychedelic exploration, Eastern spirituality, and communal living.

3. 1980s-1990s: Self-Help and Positive Psychology
The 1980s and 1990s marked the popularity of self-help literature and the positive psychology movement.

Books like "The 7 Habits of Highly Effective People" by Stephen Covey and "Awaken the Giant Within" by Tony Robbins encouraged individuals to take control of their lives, set goals, and cultivate personal empowerment.

4. 2000s-2010s: Digital Age and Self-Improvement Apps
The digital age brought self-actualization into the online sphere, with self-improvement blogs, podcasts, and apps becoming popular.

Platforms like TED Talks and mindfulness meditation apps like Headspace and Calm made personal growth resources easily accessible. Both are destined to be lampooned by future cultural historians for decades. Fulfillment? There's a Talk about that.

Actualization and peace of mind? There is an App for that. A true play on the food-fast, quick fix, hit-and-quit, unearned spiritual treasure mentality of the early-to-mid Internet Age.

5. 2010s-Present: New Traditionalism and Mindful Living
The 2010s and beyond have seen a resurgence of interest in traditional values and mindful living, often in response to the fast-paced, technology-driven world.

Concepts like minimalism, slow living, and mindfulness have gained traction, emphasizing the importance of intentional living, authenticity, and well-being.

Throughout these decades, the paradigms of self-actualization have adapted to cultural and societal shifts. The overarching theme remains a focus on personal growth, authenticity, and the pursuit of a fulfilling life. In today's world, the convergence of digital technology and timeless wisdom has created a diverse landscape for individuals seeking to realize their potential and lead meaningful lives.

The Back-to-the-Land Movement in the U.S.
1920s-1970s

There was a back-to-the-land movement in the United States during the early 20th century, although it gained more significant momentum in the 1930s as a response to the economic challenges of the Great Depression. This movement encouraged people to leave urban areas and return to rural life, often in pursuit of self-sufficiency and a simpler way of living. It was influenced by a variety of factors, including disillusionment with industrialization, the desire for more autonomy, and a romanticized view of rural living.

The back-to-the-land movement during this period saw individuals and families purchasing small farms or homesteads, growing their own food, and engaging in agricultural practices. Some of the movement's ideals aligned with the broader ethos of self-reliance and self-sufficiency that was prevalent during this time.

It's important to note that this early 20th-century back-to-the-land movement had its own unique historical context and motivations, distinct from later iterations of the movement in the 1960s and 1970s. However, it shares some common themes with these later movements, including a desire for a simpler, more authentic way of life and a rejection of urbanization and industrialization.

§

The latter-day back-to-the-land movement in the United States, which gained momentum in the late 1960s and 1970s, was closely tied to the ideals of self-actualization and personal growth. This movement was a response to the societal and cultural changes of the time, including the counterculture and environmental concerns, and it reflected a desire for a simpler, more authentic way of life.

Key aspects of the back-to-the-land movement and its connection to self-actualization include:

1. Self-Sufficiency: Many individuals and families who participated in the movement sought to live a more self-sufficient and sustainable lifestyle. They believed that by growing their own food, building their own homes, and generating their own energy, they could gain a deeper sense of autonomy and self-reliance. This quest for self-sufficiency was seen as a path to personal empowerment and growth.

2. Connection to Nature: Back-to-the-land adherents often relocated to rural areas, homesteads, or communes, embracing a closer connection to nature. This connection was seen as essential for personal well-being and self-actualization. Living in harmony with the natural world and away from the trappings of modern urban life allowed for greater introspection and a simpler, more intentional way of living.

3. Rejection of Materialism: The movement was characterized by a rejection of consumerism and materialism. Participants sought to simplify their lives, often living in small, eco-friendly dwellings and reducing their reliance on material possessions. This shift in values reflected a desire to focus on personal growth and inner fulfillment rather than external acquisitions.

4. Community and Communal Living: Many back-to-the-land communities emphasized communal living and shared resources. Living in close-knit communities fostered a sense of belonging, cooperation, and mutual support. These communal environments provided opportunities for personal growth through interpersonal relationships and shared responsibilities.

5. Alternative Values and Spirituality: The movement often embraced alternative spiritual beliefs, such as Eastern philosophies, Native American spirituality, or a deep reverence for the Earth. These spiritual perspectives encouraged self-exploration, mindfulness, and a quest for higher consciousness.

6. Environmental Consciousness: Back-to-the-land adherents were often pioneers in the modern environmental movement. Their commitment to sustainable agriculture, renewable energy, and conservation reflected a deep concern for the planet and a belief that personal growth and self-actualization were intertwined with the health of the Earth.

The back-to-the-land movement exemplified a quest for personal fulfillment, authenticity, and self-actualization by rejecting societal norms and pursuing a simpler, more connected, and sustainable way of life. While the movement waned in the late 1970s, its legacy continues to influence modern sustainability movements and those seeking a deeper sense of self and purpose through a closer relationship with nature and community.

The New Traditionalism in the U.S.
2020-2024

The movement in the United States where people and communities are returning to traditional values encompasses various aspects of life and reflects a desire for a simpler, more grounded, and values-based existence. This movement has gained traction in response to the fast-paced, technologically driven modern world. Some key facets of this movement include:

1. Homesteading and Self-Sufficiency: Many individuals and families are embracing homesteading and self-sufficiency practices, such as growing their own food, raising livestock, and preserving traditional skills like canning and fermenting. This return to agrarian traditions allows people to reconnect with the land, reduce reliance on commercial systems, and foster a sense of self-reliance.

2. Minimalism and Sustainable Living: The minimalist movement encourages a deliberate reduction in material possessions and a focus on quality over quantity. It aligns with traditional values of frugality and simplicity, emphasizing the importance of living within one's means and reducing waste. Sustainable living practices, such as reducing energy consumption and minimizing environmental impact, also tie into these values.

3. Localism and Community Building: There is a growing emphasis on supporting local businesses and communities. People are seeking to strengthen connections with neighbors, foster a sense of belonging, and build resilient local economies. This trend has led to the resurgence of farmers' markets, local artisanal products, and community initiatives.

4. Traditional Crafts and Artisanal Skills: Interest in traditional crafts and artisanal skills, such as woodworking, blacksmithing, pottery, and textile arts, is on the rise. Communities are reviving these skills through workshops, classes, and apprenticeships, preserving cultural heritage and promoting a sense of craftsmanship.

5. Alternative Education: Some families are turning to alternative education models like homeschooling or Montessori education, which often align with traditional values of parental involvement in education, individualized learning, and a focus on character development.

6. Faith-Based Communities: Traditional religious and faith-based communities continue to play a central role in preserving and passing on traditional values, emphasizing moral and ethical principles, and providing a sense of belonging and support.

7. Cultural Revival: There is a renewed interest in preserving cultural traditions, including indigenous practices, languages, and ceremonies. This revival seeks to honor and preserve cultural heritage and connect individuals to their roots.

8. Mental Health and Wellness: Traditional practices like mindfulness, meditation, and herbal medicine are gaining popularity as people seek holistic approaches to health and well-being.

The movement toward returning to traditional values is driven by a desire for authenticity, a deeper sense of purpose, and a rejection of the hyper-consumerism and disconnection often associated with modern life. It seeks to balance the benefits of technological advancements with the timeless wisdom of traditional values, fostering a richer, more meaningful, and sustainable way of life.

§

Larry's Individual Way

We return to the fact that Larry Darrell is not one that runs with the pack. He is the lone wolf.

Larry Darrell's spiritual search in W. Somerset Maugham's novel "The Razor's Edge" and the back-to-the-land movement or return to traditionalism share some common themes, as well as notable differences:

Common Themes:

1. Simplicity and Authenticity: Both Larry's spiritual search and the back-to-the-land movement emphasize the importance of simplicity and authenticity. They reject materialism and seek more meaningful, grounded lives.

2. Connection to Nature: Larry's spiritual journey often takes him to natural and serene settings, reflecting a connection to nature that parallels the back-to-the-land movement's focus on sustainable living and harmony with the environment.

3. Self-Reliance: Both Larry and those returning to traditional values value self-reliance. Larry seeks to understand and improve himself independently, while proponents of traditionalism often embrace self-sufficiency and skill-building.

4. Rejection of Conventional Norms: Larry's rejection of societal conventions and the back-to-the-land movement's departure from mainstream consumerism reflect a shared desire to break free from societal norms and expectations.

Notable Differences:

1. Spiritual vs. Lifestyle Focus: Larry's search is primarily a spiritual quest for deeper understanding and enlightenment. In contrast, the back-to-the-land movement is often more focused on lifestyle choices, such as sustainable farming and communal living.

2. Community vs. Individualism: The back-to-the-land movement often involves communal living and a sense of shared purpose, while Larry's journey is more individualistic, marked by his personal exploration.

3. Time Period: Larry's story is set in the early 20th century, while the back-to-the-land movement gained prominence in the late 1960s and 1970s. These different time periods reflect distinct cultural and societal contexts.

4. Spiritual vs. Practical Skills: Larry's spiritual journey involves encounters with mystics and deep philosophical exploration. In contrast, the back-to-the-land movement often focuses on acquiring practical skills like farming, carpentry, and sustainable living practices. This last difference I find most unappealing of the lot.

In summary, while both Larry's spiritual search and the back-to-the-land movement share some core values, such as simplicity and a rejection of materialism, they differ in their primary focus, community dynamics, and the specific skills or knowledge they prioritize. Larry's journey is more about personal transformation and understanding, while the back-to-the-land movement is often centered on lifestyle choices and sustainability.

§

The decision to join an intentional spiritual community or pursue a solo spiritual path depends on individual preferences, goals, and circumstances. Here's a comparison and contrast of these two approaches.

Joining an Intentional Spiritual Community

Pros:

1. Community Support: Spiritual communities offer a built-in support system of like-minded individuals who share similar beliefs and practices. This support can be invaluable in times of spiritual or personal challenges.

2. Guidance and Mentorship: Many spiritual communities have experienced leaders or teachers who can provide guidance, instruction, and mentorship, accelerating one's spiritual growth.

3. Structured Environment: Spiritual communities often provide a structured environment for practice, study, and rituals, which can help maintain discipline and focus.

4. Shared Resources: Communities may pool resources for communal living, reducing individual costs and enabling members to focus more on spiritual pursuits.

Cons:

1. Loss of Autonomy: Joining a community may require adhering to communal rules and norms, which could limit personal autonomy and decision-making.

2. Conflict and Dogma: Spiritual communities can sometimes become insular or dogmatic, leading to conflicts or a stifling of individual creativity and exploration.

3. Dependency: There is a risk of becoming overly dependent on the community for emotional or financial support, which can hinder personal growth and self-reliance.

Going It Alone on a Solo Spiritual Path

Pros:

1. Independence: Solo spiritual practitioners have complete autonomy over their spiritual journey, allowing for exploration and experimentation without external constraints.

2. Personalized Path: A solo path can be customized to suit individual beliefs and preferences, allowing for a more personal and unique spiritual experience.

3. Self-Discovery: Going it alone often involves greater self-discovery and self-reliance, as individuals must navigate their spiritual journey independently.

Cons:

1. Lack of Support: Solo practitioners may miss the support, camaraderie, and guidance that come with belonging to a spiritual community.

2. Isolation: Solitude can lead to feelings of isolation, and individuals may struggle to find like-minded individuals to share their experiences with.

3. Limited Resources: Some resources, such as teachings, rituals, or spaces for meditation, may be less accessible to solo practitioners.

Ultimately, the choice between joining an intentional spiritual community and pursuing a solo path depends on individual preferences and needs. Some may thrive in a communal environment with shared beliefs, while others may find deeper meaning and self-discovery on a solitary journey. Some individuals may even choose a hybrid approach, combining periods of solo practice with participation in spiritual communities as they see fit.

Week 9:
Comparative Analysis

Stumbling Up the Mountain:
"The Razor's Edge" and "The Guide" by R.K. Narayan

"The Razor's Edge" by W. Somerset Maugham and "The Guide" by R.K. Narayan are two novels that explore the themes of spiritual seeking, self-discovery, and the search for meaning in life. While they share some common themes, they differ in terms of setting, narrative style, and cultural context. Here's a comparison of the two:

Setting and Cultural Context:

1. "The Razor's Edge" (1944): Maugham's novel is set in the aftermath of World War I and primarily takes place in Europe, the United States, and India. The story delves into the experiences of Western characters who seek spiritual enlightenment, with India serving as a significant backdrop for their journeys.

2. "The Guide" (1958): Narayan's novel is set in the fictional town of Malgudi, which is a recurring setting in many of his works. "The Guide" explores the life of Raju, an ordinary man in a small Indian town, whose life takes an unexpected turn when he becomes a spiritual guide.

Narrative Style and Structure:

1. "The Razor's Edge": Maugham employs a first-person narrative style, where the author himself serves as a character in the story. This allows Maugham to provide his perspective on the characters and their spiritual journeys. The novel is structured as a series of interconnected stories, each focusing on different characters.

2. "The Guide": Narayan's novel is written in the third person and follows a more traditional narrative structure. It provides insight into the thoughts and actions of the protagonist, Raju, as he navigates his life's twists and turns.

Themes:

1. Spiritual Seeking: Both novels explore the theme of spiritual seeking and self-discovery. In "The Razor's Edge," characters like Larry Darrell and Sophie Macdonald embark on spiritual journeys in the aftermath of World War I. In "The Guide," Raju's transformation into a spiritual guide forms the core of the narrative.

2. Cultural and Philosophical Differences: "The Razor's Edge" delves into the clash of Western and Eastern philosophies, particularly in the Indian context. It highlights the influence of Eastern spirituality on Western characters. In contrast, "The Guide" is firmly rooted in Indian culture and spirituality, with a focus on Hinduism and the concept of dharma.

Character Development:

1. "The Razor's Edge": Maugham's novel features a diverse cast of characters, each on their own spiritual journey. Larry Darrell, in particular, undergoes significant personal growth and self-discovery.

2. "The Guide": "The Guide" primarily follows the transformation of Raju, a seemingly ordinary man who becomes entangled in a web of spirituality, fraud, and redemption.

In summary, while both novels explore spiritual seeking and self-discovery, they differ in terms of setting, narrative style, and cultural context. "The Razor's Edge" is a more expansive and interconnected narrative with a Western perspective on Eastern spirituality, while "The Guide" is firmly rooted in Indian culture and explores the journey of a single protagonist. Both novels, however, offer valuable insights into the human quest for meaning and enlightenment.

§

Self Deception and Unhappy Endings:
"The Razor's Edge" and Kipling's "The Man Who Would Be King"

"The Razor's Edge" by W. Somerset Maugham and "The Man Who Would Be King" by Rudyard Kipling both touch upon the theme of self-deception and the consequences that arise from it, but they approach this theme in distinct ways:

"The Razor's Edge":

1. Self-Deception: In "The Razor's Edge," the character Elliott Templeton embodies self-deception. He is a socialite who clings to the trappings of the upper class, despite the emptiness of his life.

He deceives himself into believing that his shallow pursuits are meaningful and important.

2. Consequences: The consequences of Elliott's self-deception are a sense of isolation and a failure to achieve true happiness. He remains trapped in a world of social appearances and never experiences the personal growth and fulfillment that come from self-awareness and authenticity.

3. Larry Darrell: In contrast, the protagonist Larry Darrell is on a quest for self-discovery and enlightenment. He rejects societal expectations and pursues a path of spiritual seeking. His journey leads to personal growth and a deeper understanding of life.

"The Man Who Would Be King":

1. Self-Deception: In "The Man Who Would Be King," the two protagonists, Daniel Dravot and Peachey Carnehan, are British adventurers who deceive themselves into thinking they can establish themselves as kings among the indigenous people of Afghanistan. They believe they can control and exploit the situation without considering the potential consequences.

2. Consequences: The consequences of their self-deception are severe. Their grandiose ambitions lead to a tragic and violent downfall. They underestimate the complexities of the local culture and overestimate their own abilities. Their self-deception ultimately results in betrayal, loss of trust, and dire consequences.

3. Cultural Misunderstanding: Another aspect of self-deception in the novella is the protagonists' misunderstanding of the indigenous culture and their belief in their superiority. Their ignorance of local customs and traditions leads to misunderstandings and a breakdown in their plans.

In both novels, self-deception has consequences that affect the characters' lives and their interactions with others. While Larry Darrell's journey in "The Razor's Edge" ultimately leads to personal growth and enlightenment, the self-deception of Dravot and Carnehan in "The Man Who Would Be King" leads to tragedy and a stark reminder of the dangers of overestimating one's abilities and underestimating the complexities of other cultures.

§

The Darkness Beckons:
"The Razor's Edge" and "Les Fleurs du Mal" (Flowers of Evil) by Charles Baudelaire

"The Razor's Edge" by W. Somerset Maugham and "Les Fleurs du Mal" (Flowers of Evil) by Charles Baudelaire are two works of literature that explore themes of inner turmoil, decadence, and the human condition. While they belong to different genres and were written in different eras, there are some thematic parallels, and we can draw comparisons between Sophie in "The Razor's Edge" and the themes in "Flowers of Evil":

Sophie in "The Razor's Edge"

1. Character Background: Sophie Macdonald is a complex character in "The Razor's Edge." She is a wealthy and beautiful woman who struggles with inner demons, including alcoholism and the trauma of losing her husband and child during World War I.

2. Decadence and Despair: Sophie's character embodies a sense of decadence and despair. Her self-destructive behavior, including heavy drinking and promiscuity, reflects a sense of emptiness and disillusionment with the world.

3. Search for Redemption: Sophie's character embarks on a quest for redemption and meaning in her life. She seeks solace in spiritual pursuits and, at times, attempts to overcome her personal demons.

Themes in "Flowers of Evil" by Charles Baudelaire

1. Decadence: "Flowers of Evil" is a collection of poetry that explores themes of decadence, moral decline, and the darker aspects of human nature. Baudelaire's poems often depict the allure of sin and the hedonistic tendencies of society.

2. Inner Turmoil: Many of Baudelaire's poems delve into the inner turmoil and conflict within the human psyche. He explores the duality of human nature, where desires and vices often clash with societal norms.

3. Search for Transcendence: Despite the darkness and decadence depicted in his poems, Baudelaire also expresses a desire for transcendence and escape from the mundane. He seeks beauty, art, and moments of ecstasy amid the chaos of existence.

Comparisons

1. Decadence and Inner Turmoil: Both Sophie's character in "The Razor's Edge" and the themes in "Flowers of Evil" touch on themes of decadence and inner turmoil. Sophie's struggles and self-destructive tendencies parallel the darker aspects of human nature explored by Baudelaire.

2. Search for Meaning: In both works, there is a quest for meaning and redemption. Sophie seeks solace and healing, while Baudelaire's poems often grapple with the search for transcendence amid the chaos of life.

3. Exploration of the Human Condition: Both Maugham and Baudelaire delve into the complexities of the human condition. They depict characters and themes that reflect the fragility, desires, and conflicts within the human psyche.

In summary, while Sophie in "The Razor's Edge" is a specific character with her own narrative arc, she shares thematic connections with the exploration of decadence and the search for meaning found in Charles Baudelaire's "Flowers of Evil." Both works delve into the complexities of human nature and the challenges individuals face in navigating their inner struggles.

§

Trauma and Transformation: "The Razor's Edge" and "Wild" by Cheryl Strayed

"Wild" by Cheryl Strayed and "The Razor's Edge" by W. Somerset Maugham both depict transformative journeys, but they differ in terms of their protagonists, motivations, and the nature of their quests. Here's a comparison and contrast of Larry's journey in "The Razor's Edge" and Cheryl's journey in "Wild":

Larry's Journey in "The Razor's Edge" (Larry Darrell)

Protagonist: Larry Darrell is a thoughtful and introspective World War I veteran who embarks on a spiritual quest to find meaning and enlightenment in life.

Motivation: Larry's quest is driven by a deep sense of disillusionment with the materialism and shallowness of Western society. He seeks answers to profound existential questions and a higher understanding of existence.

Nature of Quest: Larry's journey is primarily spiritual and philosophical. He travels to Europe and India, immersing himself in Eastern spirituality and seeking guidance from gurus and mystics. His quest involves introspection, meditation, and the pursuit of inner peace.

Transformation: Over the course of the novel, Larry undergoes a significant transformation. He gains wisdom, a sense of detachment from worldly desires, and a deep understanding of the human condition. His quest leads to personal growth and enlightenment.

Cheryl's Journey in "Wild" (Cheryl Strayed)

Protagonist: Cheryl Strayed is a young woman who embarks on a solo hiking journey along the Pacific Crest Trail after experiencing personal tragedies and emotional turmoil.

Motivation: Cheryl's journey is motivated by a desire to heal from the pain of her mother's death, a failed marriage, and a period of self-destructive behavior. She seeks redemption and a fresh start in life.

Nature of Quest: Cheryl's journey is physical and psychological. She embarks on a grueling hike through the wilderness, facing physical challenges and confronting her emotional scars along the way. Her quest involves survival, self-discovery, and personal catharsis.

Transformation: Throughout her journey, Cheryl experiences physical hardship and emotional catharsis. She gains self-reliance, resilience, and a sense of inner strength. Her quest leads to personal healing and a new sense of purpose.

Comparison and Contrast:

Motivation: Larry's motivation is primarily spiritual and philosophical, driven by a search for existential meaning. Cheryl's motivation is more personal and emotional, rooted in the need to overcome specific traumas and find emotional healing.

Nature of Quest: Larry's quest is focused on meditation, spiritual teachings, and inner peace, while Cheryl's quest is centered on physical endurance, survival, and confronting personal demons.

Transformation: Both characters undergo significant transformations, but their journeys lead to different forms of growth. Larry finds spiritual enlightenment and detachment, while Cheryl finds emotional healing and self-empowerment.

Setting: Larry's journey takes him to Europe and India, while Cheryl's journey is set along the Pacific Crest Trail in the United States. The settings reflect the different cultural and geographical contexts of their quests.

In summary, while both "The Razor's Edge" and "Wild" depict transformative journeys, they differ in terms of their protagonists' motivations, the nature of their quests, and the types of growth and healing they achieve. Larry's quest is more spiritual and philosophical, while Cheryl's is a blend of physical and psychological challenges on her path to personal catharsis and healing.

§

Cross-Cultural Perspectives on Self-Realization

Self-Actualization and Enlightenment are complex concepts with varying definitions across different cultures and time periods. Here are examples of what these terms have meant to people in various traditions:

1. U.K. (Western Enlightenment):
Self-Actualization: In Western thought, self-actualization often refers to the realization of one's full potential and personal growth. It may involve achieving goals, pursuing passions, and attaining a sense of fulfillment.

Enlightenment: The Western Enlightenment of the 17th and 18th centuries emphasized reason, science, and individual liberty. It sought to free society from ignorance, superstition, and oppressive institutions through rational thought and inquiry.

2. European Traditions:
Self-Actualization: In European contexts, self-actualization may relate to personal achievement, intellectual development, and self-

expression. It can also encompass the pursuit of happiness and well-being.

Enlightenment: European Enlightenment emphasized reason, secularism, and humanism. It aimed to challenge traditional authority and promote intellectual and social progress.

3. Russian Traditions:
Self-Actualization: Russian thought often includes an emphasis on moral and spiritual growth. Self-actualization may involve inner transformation, moral integrity, and connection to the collective.

Enlightenment: Russian Enlightenment in the 18th century sought to modernize and educate society. It focused on European ideals but incorporated Russian cultural and religious elements.

4. Pacific Island Traditions:
Self-Actualization: In Pacific Island cultures, self-actualization may involve preserving cultural heritage, maintaining harmony with nature, and achieving communal well-being.

Enlightenment: Enlightenment in Pacific Island cultures often relates to spiritual insight, traditional knowledge, and wisdom passed down through oral traditions.

5. Latin American Traditions:
Self-Actualization: Latin American self-actualization may encompass identity, cultural preservation, and social justice. It often involves a quest for dignity, equality, and empowerment.

Enlightenment: Latin American Enlightenment in the 18th century was influenced by European ideals but was intertwined with colonial struggles. It emphasized independence, democracy, and social reform.

6. Asian Traditions:
Self-Actualization: In Asian cultures, self-actualization may involve spiritual awakening, meditation, and achieving inner peace. It often connects personal development with collective well-being.

Enlightenment: Asian enlightenment can relate to spiritual enlightenment, such as achieving nirvana in Buddhism, or gaining wisdom and insight through philosophical or religious practices.

7. Present-Day Global Perspectives:

Present-day definitions of self-actualization in Asia, the Pacific Islands, and South America are influenced by cultural, social, and individual factors unique to each region. While there can be variations within these regions, here are general understandings of self-actualization in each:

Asia

Self-actualization in Asian cultures often emphasizes a holistic approach to personal development and well-being, including physical, mental, and spiritual dimensions. It may include:

1. Spiritual Growth: Many Asians seek self-actualization through spiritual practices like meditation, mindfulness, and yoga. This involves achieving inner peace, enlightenment, and a deeper connection to the self and the universe.

2. Harmony and Balance: Asians often value balance and harmony in life, striving for equilibrium between work, family, and personal interests. Achieving this balance is considered a form of self-actualization.

3. Fulfillment of Duty: Some Asian cultures place importance on fulfilling one's duty to family, society, and tradition. Self-actualization can involve living up to these responsibilities while also pursuing personal goals.

4. Cultural Identity: For many Asians, self-actualization involves a strong connection to cultural identity and heritage. This may include preserving traditional practices and values while adapting to a changing world.

Pacific Islands

In Pacific Island cultures, self-actualization is often closely tied to communal well-being, cultural preservation, and maintaining harmony with nature. It may encompass:

1. Cultural Preservation: Self-actualization involves preserving and passing down cultural traditions, oral histories, and indigenous knowledge to future generations.

2. Environmental Stewardship: Many Pacific Islanders have a deep connection to their natural surroundings. Self-actualization includes responsible stewardship of the environment and maintaining a harmonious relationship with nature.

3. Community Engagement: Being actively involved in one's community and contributing to its well-being is a form of self-actualization. This includes participating in communal activities and supporting local initiatives.

4. Social Justice: Some Pacific Islanders view self-actualization as advocating for social justice, particularly in contexts where colonial histories and external influences have created disparities.

South America

Self-actualization in South America often involves personal growth and cultural identity. Key aspects include:

1. Cultural Expression: South Americans often find self-actualization in expressing their cultural identity through art, music, dance, and storytelling. This fosters a sense of belonging and pride.

2. Spirituality and Connection: Some South American cultures have deep spiritual traditions, such as indigenous beliefs or syncretic practices. Self-actualization involves spiritual connection, often linked to nature and ancestral wisdom.

3. Personal Fulfillment: Like other regions, South Americans also pursue personal growth, education, and well-being as part of self-actualization. It may involve pursuing passions, achieving goals, and finding a sense of purpose.

It's important to note that these definitions are broad and can vary significantly within and between countries and cultures. Individuals within these regions may have unique interpretations of self-actualization based on their personal beliefs, experiences, and circumstances.

These definitions and examples are provided in an effort to highlight the diversity of meanings associated with self-actualization and enlightenment across different cultures and time periods, reflecting the rich tapestry of human experiences and aspirations, and is by no means comprehensive.

§

Group Encounters:
Modern Interpretations of Self-Actualization in the U.S.

1. Human Potential Movement:
The Human Potential Movement, which gained prominence in the 1960s and 1970s, emphasized the development of human potential and personal growth. It encouraged individuals to explore their inner selves, develop self-awareness, and reach their fullest potential through various practices and therapies. While it had a positive impact on personal development for many, critics argued that it could be overly individualistic and self-centered, potentially neglecting broader societal concerns.

2. Self-Improvement Gurus:
Self-help and self-improvement industries have flourished in the modern era, with motivational speakers and authors offering guidance on achieving success, happiness, and personal fulfillment. While these resources can provide valuable insights and motivation, critics argue that some self-help gurus oversimplify complex issues and may promote unrealistic expectations.

3. Cults and Extreme Movements:
Some movements and groups that claim to promote self-actualization have been criticized for exploiting vulnerable individuals and engaging in manipulative practices. Certain cults and organizations have used self-actualization rhetoric to control and manipulate followers, leading to adverse effects on individuals and their well-being.

4. The "Me" Generation:
The term "Me Generation" has been used to describe generations, particularly the Baby Boomers, who are perceived as self-focused and individualistic. Critics argue that excessive focus on individual success and self-interest can lead to social fragmentation and a lack of concern for broader societal issues.

5. The Poseur Generation 2010-
Wearing all the entrapments of enlightenment and righteousness without the learning, experience, work or commitment that was required in previous generations, usually with the sole intent of appearing enlightened or diminishing another's individual, usually traditional, beliefs. A groupthink delusional mind virus that includes going to yoga, flying political flags in the front yard, watching TED talks, APPS, Electric Cars, 10,000 steps, shouting on

social media, being terrorized by FOMO (the fear of missing out) a dislike for traditional wisdom, values, art and literature and a fanatical aversion to meaningful, rational, informed discourse.

Not to make a single judgment on any of the above, but all facets of an easily lampooned presentation of self as the Preppie, Yuppie, Punk, Hippie, Sloane, Chad, Valley Girl, Mod or Hipster, and completely at odds with the path of individual spiritual searching as embodied by Larry Darrell.

§

Dangers of Racing After Self-Actualization

With the above in mind, it should be noted that critics of extreme individualism and a sole focus on self-actualization raise several concerns:

1. Social Fragmentation: Overemphasis on individualism can lead to a lack of social cohesion and a sense of community. When individuals prioritize their own goals and interests to the exclusion of others, it can result in disconnection and isolation.

2. Consumerism: Some self-improvement movements and industries are criticized for promoting consumerism, as individuals are encouraged to buy products and services in pursuit of personal growth and happiness.

3. Narcissism: An excessive focus on the self can sometimes lead to narcissistic behaviors and a lack of empathy for others. Critics argue that a self-centered approach can be detrimental to interpersonal relationships and society as a whole.

4. Neglect of Societal Issues: Critics contend that individuals who are solely focused on their own self-actualization may neglect broader societal issues such as clean water, practical education, traditional understanding of community responsibility and governance, alternative and appropriate technologies and food production techniques, and decentralized community well-being.

However, it's important to note that not all interpretations of self-actualization or self-improvement lead to these adverse effects.

Many individuals find personal growth and fulfillment through self-awareness and development. The key is to strike a balance between personal growth and a sense of social responsibility and community engagement.

Ultimately, whether self-actualization has a demoralizing and fragmenting effect on individuals and society depends on how it is pursued and integrated into one's life. A healthy approach to self-actualization considers the well-being of both the individual and the broader community, recognizing the interconnectedness of personal and societal growth. Balancing personal development with social consciousness can lead to more meaningful and sustainable forms of self-actualization.

§

And, in the most extreme, Anti-Poseur Generation move, embarking on a solitary life in the wilderness, akin to a hermit's existence, may appear idyllic and romantically appealing. Yet, beneath the surface, it harbors a multitude of inherent perils and obstacles that demand careful consideration.

Choosing a solitary life in the wilderness, like a hermit, may appear alluring and romantic, but it comes with a host of inherent dangers and challenges that should not be underestimated. It's vital to recognize these risks before embarking on such a venture. To wit:

1. Isolation and Loneliness: Extended solitude can lead to profound feelings of isolation and loneliness, which can negatively impact mental and emotional well-being. Humans are social beings, and isolation can result in depression.

2. Lack of Safety Nets: Being alone in the wilderness means there's no immediate help available in emergencies. Injuries, illnesses, or accidents can become life-threatening without access to medical assistance.

3. Limited Resources: Self-sufficiency is essential for wilderness survival, and resources like food, water, and shelter may be scarce. Sustaining oneself long-term can be exceedingly challenging.

4. Harsh Environmental Conditions: The wilderness can expose individuals to extreme weather, natural disasters, and encounters with wildlife, posing risks to safety and survival.

5. Mental Health Challenges: Isolation and the absence of external stimuli can lead to mental health challenges, including anxiety, hallucinations, and emotional vulnerability.

6. Lack of Skills and Knowledge: Survival in the wilderness requires specific skills, such as navigation and wilderness first aid. A lack of these skills can lead to dangerous situations.

7. Emotional Struggles: Extended solitude can lead to introspection and emotional difficulties, making some individuals confront unresolved issues.

8. Legal Issues: Living in the wilderness without permission may result in legal and regulatory problems, including trespassing or environmental violations.

9. Sustainability Challenges: Maintaining a sustainable and self-sufficient lifestyle in the wilderness is demanding, requiring careful planning and resource management.

10. Reintegration Difficulties: Returning to society after solitude can be challenging, with potential struggles in readjusting to social interactions and daily life. Reintegration into society after an extended solitary sojourn can prove daunting, challenging one's ability to readjust to the demands of social interactions and everyday life.

To undertake this path safely and with foresight, comprehensive preparation, guidance from experts, and dependable communication for emergencies are essential.

See:

Kerouac's 'Desolation Angels' (1965): Beat wanderers, existential quest, literary exploration in post-war America. On the road to self-discovery without going completely nuts on the side of a mountain all alone.

Krakauer's 'Into the Wild' (1996): Exploration, disillusionment, and tragedy in the wilderness. A gripping tale of a young adventurer's journey.

Desolation Mountain, 1950s

In the 1950s, perched atop Desolation Mountain, a solitary fire lookout stood sentinel. With panoramic views, its watchful eyes scanned the wilderness, safeguarding against forest fires. Isolation was the price, yet the lookout's vigilance played a crucial role in preserving the untouched beauty of this pristine landscape.

Week 10-12:

Student Presentations, Discussion and Debate, and Final Research Papers

**Intentionally left Blank
for the User of this Book to
fill-in as they
see fit**

Cathedral of St. Paul, completed in 1928

Princeton University's iconic Cathedral of St. Paul, also known as the Princeton University Chapel, is a masterpiece of Gothic Revival architecture. Completed in 1928, it boasts stunning stained glass windows, intricate stone carvings, and a soaring tower that can be seen from afar.

In "The Razor's Edge", only Elliott Templeton attended university. Elliott is portrayed as a socialite and art collector who was educated at Eton and then went on to study at Oxford University. His education and social status play a significant role in his character's background and interactions within the novel.

Two "What If" Scenarios

What If Larry Had Studied with a Mystic in Paris?

He might have met George Ivanovich Gurdjief in 1925.

George Ivanovich Gurdjieff, a spiritual teacher and mystic, taught his system of spiritual development and self-awareness known as the "Fourth Way" during the early to mid-20th century. He was active as a teacher from roughly the early 1900s until his death in 1949. Gurdjieff's teachings emphasized self-observation, self-discipline, and the pursuit of higher consciousness as a means of personal transformation. His ideas and practices influenced a number of spiritual and philosophical movements, and they continue to have an impact on various spiritual seekers and groups today.

In 1925, George Gurdjieff was primarily based in France. He had established the Institute for the Harmonious Development of Man (commonly known as the Prieuré) in Fontainebleau-Avon, near Paris, which served as a center for his teachings and practices. This was a significant period in Gurdjieff's teaching career, as he had a growing number of students and followers who were studying his system of spiritual development, often referred to as the "Work" or the "Fourth Way."

During this time, Gurdjieff conducted a series of lectures, meetings, and movements (a form of sacred dance) that were integral to his teaching method. His teachings and the activities at the Prieuré attracted individuals from various backgrounds who were interested in his unique approach to self-realization and personal transformation.

George Gurdjieff's teachings, often referred to as the "Fourth Way," emphasized self-awareness, self-development, and the pursuit of higher consciousness. These teachings had certain aspects that could have been of interest to a seeker like Larry Darrell, as they complemented his quest for spiritual enlightenment. Here's what Gurdjieff could have taught Larry Darrell:

1. Self-Observation: Gurdjieff stressed the importance of self-observation and self-awareness as a means of understanding one's mechanical behavior and thought patterns. This practice of self-observation can lead to greater self-understanding and personal growth, which aligns with Larry Darrell's journey of self-discovery.

2. Work on Inner Transformation: Gurdjieff's system involved inner work, which could include practices like meditation, self-inquiry, and mindfulness. These techniques can help individuals develop a deeper connection with their inner selves, a goal that Larry Darrell was pursuing in his quest for truth.

3. Integration of Mind, Body, and Emotions: Gurdjieff emphasized the importance of harmonizing the mind, body, and emotions to achieve greater awareness and self-mastery. This holistic approach to personal development could have resonated with Larry Darrell's pursuit of a balanced and meaningful life.

4. Understanding of Human Nature: Gurdjieff's teachings explored the idea of different levels of consciousness and the fragmented nature of human psychology. This understanding could have provided Larry Darrell with insights into the complexities of human nature and behavior.

Regarding portability, Gurdjieff's teachings were not tied to a specific religious or cultural tradition. They were designed to be adaptable and practical for individuals from diverse backgrounds. Gurdjieff believed that one could pursue self-development and spiritual awakening while remaining engaged in everyday life. This aspect of his teaching made it more portable and accessible compared to some traditional religious disciplines that might require strict adherence to specific rituals or dogmas.

However, it's important to note that Gurdjieff's teachings were also known for their intensity and demands on the practitioner. The "Work" required a serious commitment and a willingness to confront one's own limitations and weaknesses. Whether Larry Darrell would have found Gurdjieff's teachings more suitable or effective than what he learned in India is a matter of conjecture, as it depends on his individual preferences and experiences on his spiritual journey. The fictional character of Larry Darrell in "The Razor's Edge" ultimately chooses his own path to enlightenment, which may or may not align with Gurdjieff's teachings.

He certainly would not have been the submissive type, ready to endure some of the self-style Western Guru's methods. Gurdjieff, had a complex personality and teaching style, which led to a range of opinions and complaints from his students and associates. While some of his students were deeply devoted to him and his teachings, others had criticisms and complaints. Here are some common complaints and criticisms that have been raised by Gurdjieff's students and associates:

1. Authoritarianism: Gurdjieff was known for his strong, often authoritarian, teaching style. Some students found his approach to be harsh and demanding, with strict rules and discipline. They felt that he could be domineering and controlling.

2. Secrecy: Gurdjieff was known to be secretive about certain aspects of his teachings, and he often revealed information to students on a need-to-know basis. Some students felt frustrated by this secrecy and a lack of transparency in his teachings.

3. Financial Demands: Gurdjieff's teaching centers and groups often required students to make financial contributions, and some students felt that the cost of participating in his teachings was burdensome.

4. Physical Rigors: Gurdjieff introduced physical exercises and movements as part of his teaching method, and some students found these exercises physically demanding and challenging.

5. Unconventional Methods: Gurdjieff's teaching methods were unconventional and often aimed at shocking students out of their ordinary state of consciousness. This could be unsettling and uncomfortable for some.

6. Inconsistent Behavior: Some students noted that Gurdjieff's behavior could be inconsistent and unpredictable, making it difficult to understand his intentions or teachings.

7. Cultural Insensitivity: Gurdjieff's use of different cultural and religious elements in his teaching materials led to accusations of cultural insensitivity or appropriation by some students.

It's important to note that Gurdjieff's teaching had a significant impact on many of his students, and some were deeply devoted to him and his ideas. They saw value in the challenges and demands of his teaching style and believed it led to personal transformation. Others, however, were critical of various aspects of his approach.

These complaints and criticisms reflect the diversity of experiences within Gurdjieff's circle of students and associates and illustrate the complexities of his teachings and personality. Gurdjieff remains a controversial figure in the realm of spirituality and mysticism, with both fervent supporters and vocal detractors.

All in all, it seems like Larry was lucky not to run into this character. Plus, Maugham already presented his portrait of Aleister Crowley, a much different type of malevolent occultist in "The Magician," published in 1908.

What if Larry had just gone to a library and studied the Christian mystics?

In 1925, Larry Darrell, if he were exploring Christian mysticism in a European or UK seminary, would have had access to a range of books and writings that could have informed his spiritual development.

These books would have offered various perspectives, some complementary to his lessons in India and others potentially adversarial or contrasting. Here are some notable texts that he might have encountered:

Complementary Texts:

1. "The Cloud of Unknowing": This anonymous medieval English work is a classic of Christian mysticism, emphasizing contemplative prayer and the pursuit of union with God through the "cloud of unknowing."

2. "The Interior Castle" by Teresa of Ávila: A seminal work in Catholic mysticism, Teresa of Ávila's book explores the stages of the soul's journey toward union with God, often referred to as the "seven mansions."

3. "The Dark Night of the Soul" by John of the Cross: This work by the Spanish mystic John of the Cross delves into the soul's journey through spiritual darkness and purification on the path to divine union.

4. "Revelations of Divine Love" by Julian of Norwich: Julian of Norwich's writings, particularly her "Showings," offer insights into God's love and the soul's connection to the divine.

Adversarial or Contrasting Texts:

1. "The Varieties of Religious Experience" by William James:
This influential psychological and philosophical work examines
religious and mystical experiences across different traditions,
providing a more analytical perspective.

2. "The Life of Reason" by George Santayana: Santayana's work
is secular in nature but explores the philosophical dimensions of
human experience, including spirituality and mysticism.

3. "Mysticism and Logic" by Bertrand Russell: Russell's essay
addresses mysticism from a philosophical and critical standpoint,
questioning its validity and the nature of mystical experiences.

§

**There are a few Texts that might not directly conflict with the
Indian Teachings, while remaining profoundly Christian.**

Christian mysticism encompasses a wide range of writings and
traditions, and while many of these texts emphasize similar
spiritual themes to those found in Eastern spirituality, there are
also Christian classics that may present contrasting or adversarial
perspectives to the lessons Larry learned in India. Here are a few
Christian classics that, while primarily mystical, might differ in
certain aspects:

1. "The Imitation of Christ" by Thomas à Kempis: This classic
work of Christian mysticism focuses on the imitation of Christ's
life and teachings, emphasizing humility, self-denial, and the
pursuit of a life centered on Christ. While it shares elements of
self-transformation with Eastern spirituality, it may differ in its
emphasis on devotion to Christ as the central path.

2. "The Way of Perfection" by Teresa of Ávila: St. Teresa of
Ávila's writings are considered classics of Christian mysticism.
In "The Way of Perfection," she discusses the importance of
prayer, contemplation, and the pursuit of spiritual perfection.
Her emphasis on devotion to Christ and her Catholic theological
framework might contrast with some Eastern teachings.

3. "The Practice of the Presence of God" by Brother Lawrence: Brother Lawrence's work emphasizes the importance of continuous awareness of God's presence in everyday life. While it shares elements of mindfulness and presence with Eastern spirituality, it does so within a Christian context.

It's important to note that while these Christian mystical classics may have some differences in emphasis or theological framework when compared to lessons from Eastern spirituality, they are all part of the rich tapestry of mystical literature. Each tradition offers its own unique insights and approaches to the mystical path, and individuals like Larry Darrell might draw from a variety of sources in their quest for spiritual understanding and personal transformation.

§

Larry Darrell, in his quest for truth and enlightenment, might have encountered these texts in a seminary or through his own reading.

His journey could involve integrating insights from both Eastern and Western spiritual traditions while navigating the diverse perspectives found in the world of mysticism and spirituality.

An interesting intellectual game to play, nevertheless. Might be just as interesting to ask what he would have become if he was excellent at horsemanship, cricket or sculpture. But, we will leave questions like that for another book.

More Reading?

Yes.

Here is a list of 10 20th-century works that explore the common themes of self-actualization vs. self-delusion, including:

1. **"Rabbit, Run" by John Updike (1960):** The first book in John Updike's Rabbit Angstrom series, it follows the life of Harry "Rabbit" Angstrom as he grapples with his own self-delusions and quest for meaning.

2 **"One Flew Over the Cuckoo's Nest" by Ken Kesey (1962):** This novel features a cast of characters in a mental institution, highlighting themes of conformity, rebellion, and self-realization.

3. **"The Stranger" by Albert Camus (1942):** The protagonist Meursault's indifference to societal norms and his existential journey raise questions of self-actualization and authenticity.

4. **"Zen and the Art of Motorcycle Maintenance" by Robert M. Pirsig (1974):** The narrator's philosophical motorcycle journey explores themes of quality, rationality, and the pursuit of deeper meaning in life.

5. **"Steppenwolf" by Hermann Hesse (1927):** The novel follows Harry Haller's inner struggles as he grapples with his dual nature and seeks self-realization amidst a bourgeois society.

6. **"The Road Less Traveled" by M. Scott Peck (1978):** Although non-fiction, this book explores the themes of personal growth, self-actualization, and the importance of confronting one's own self-delusions.

7. **"Nausea" by Jean-Paul Sartre (1938):** This existentialist novel delves into the life of Antoine Roquentin, who experiences a profound existential crisis while questioning the nature of existence and authenticity.

8. "S.: A Novel" by John Updike (1988): The second Updike novel on this list explores themes of self-deception, spirituality, and the search for meaning, which can be compared to some aspects of Somerset Maugham's "The Razor's Edge."

In "S.," the protagonist, Sarah Worth, is a woman who becomes involved with a self-proclaimed guru named Kalu.

Like Larry Darrell in "The Razor's Edge," Sarah seeks spiritual fulfillment but becomes entangled with a charismatic figure. The novel delves into the complexities of Sarah's relationships and her journey toward self-realization, including her struggle with, surprise, self-deception.

While "S." and "The Razor's Edge" both explore themes of spirituality and self-deception, they do so in distinct narrative styles and cultural contexts. "S." is known for its introspective and psychological exploration of the characters' inner lives, while "The Razor's Edge" offers a broader examination of the quest for self-realization and enlightenment in a post-World War I setting.

Comparing and contrasting these two novels could provide interesting insights into the themes of self-deception and self-actualization in literature.

9. "The Assistant" by Bernard Malamud (1957): In this novel, Morris Bober, an aging Jewish grocery store owner, is at the center of the story. The novel touches on themes of economic struggle, identity, and self-deception as Bober grapples with his personal challenges and aspirations.

10. "Revolutionary Road" by Richard Yates (1961): This novel follows the lives of Frank and April Wheeler, a suburban couple who appear to have the perfect life but are deeply dissatisfied with their existence. The novel explores themes of conformity, denial, and self-deception in the context of the American Dream.

All in all, these novels offer a diverse range of perspectives on the themes of self-actualization and self-delusion, providing rich literary explorations of the human condition and the quest for meaning and authenticity.

The Films

"The Razor's Edge," based on Somerset Maugham's novel, has been adapted into film twice, with notable differences in the two adaptations. Here's a comparison and sample critical responses for each film:

1. "The Razor's Edge" (1946):

Director: Edmund Goulding.
Starring: Tyrone Power as Larry Darrell, Gene Tierney as Isabel Bradley, and Clifton Webb as Elliott Templeton.

Synopsis: This black-and-white adaptation follows the story of Larry Darrell, a World War I veteran who embarks on a journey of self-discovery and spiritual enlightenment. It explores his travels to Europe and India, his encounters with various characters, and his ultimate quest for meaning.

Critical Response:
Positive: Critics praised Tyrone Power's performance as Larry Darrell and the film's faithful adaptation of Maugham's novel. The film was considered a thoughtful exploration of themes such as self-realization and spiritual awakening.
Negative: Some critics found the pacing of the film slow, and it received mixed reviews upon its release. Some felt that the complex themes of the novel were not fully explored in the adaptation.

2. "The Razor's Edge" (1984):

Director: John Byrum.
Starring: Bill Murray as Larry Darrell, Theresa Russell as Isabel Bradley, and Catherine Hicks as Sophie MacDonald.

Synopsis: This color adaptation takes a more modern approach to the story, placing it in the aftermath of World War II. Bill Murray's portrayal of Larry Darrell differs significantly from Tyrone Power's, presenting a more laid-back and unconventional take on the character's pursuit of enlightenment.

Critical Response:
Mixed: Critical responses to the 1984 adaptation were mixed. While Bill Murray's performance was lauded for its unique interpretation of Larry Darrell, some critics found it challenging to accept Murray in a serious dramatic role.
Negative: The film's departure from the novel's timeline and character dynamics received criticism from fans of the original work. Some felt that it didn't capture the depth and complexity of Maugham's novel and that it simplified the narrative.

In summary, the two film adaptations of "The Razor's Edge" differ significantly in style and interpretation, and critical responses to both films have been mixed. The 1946 version is praised for its faithfulness to the source material, while the 1984 adaptation takes a more unconventional approach, with Bill Murray's performance as a notable departure from the traditional portrayal of Larry Darrell. Ultimately, the choice between the two adaptations may depend on one's preference for a more faithful or modern interpretation of the novel's themes.

§

Music

For "The Razor's Edge" (1984). Jack Nitzsche, score.

Jack Nitzsche (1937-2000) was a renowned composer, musician, and arranger, known for his work in film scoring. He had a notable career and contributed to various film soundtracks.

Jack Nitzsche: A Brief Bio:

Jack Nitzsche was a prolific American musician and composer known for his work in the music industry and film. He was a multi-talented artist who contributed to rock music, orchestration, and film scoring.

He worked with several prominent musicians, including Phil Spector, Neil Young, and the Rolling Stones, and was recognized for his innovative contributions to the "Wall of Sound" production technique.

In the realm of film scoring, Nitzsche collaborated on numerous films, earning accolades and awards for his compositions and arrangements.

Approach to Composition and Instrumentation:

Nitzsche's approach to film scoring was marked by versatility and adaptability. He had a keen sense of how music could enhance the emotional impact of a scene.

For "The Razor's Edge" (1984), Nitzsche crafted a score that complemented the film's themes of self-discovery and spirituality. He blended various musical elements, including orchestration and synthesizers, to create a unique and evocative soundscape.

Critical Response to the Score:

Critical response to Jack Nitzsche's score for "The Razor's Edge" was mixed. Some critics appreciated his ability to convey the film's introspective and spiritual themes through music. They found the score to be emotive and fitting for Larry Darrell's journey of self-discovery.

Others, however, felt that the score did not fully capture the depth and complexity of Somerset Maugham's novel. They found it somewhat conventional and less innovative compared to Nitzsche's other works.

In summary, Jack Nitzsche, a versatile composer and musician, brought his unique sensibilities to the score of "The Razor's Edge" (1984). While his approach was generally appreciated for its emotional resonance, opinions on the score varied among critics. Nitzsche's work in film scoring remains a significant part of his legacy in the world of music and cinema.

The Critic's Choice

Critics often point to certain orchestral compositions that convey the spiritual quest of the individual through their emotional depth and thematic richness.

Here are a few such compositions frequentaly suggested along with a short listening guide for each:

1. Gustav Mahler Symphony No. 2 in C Minor, "Resurrection"
Listening Guide: This symphony is known for its exploration of themes related to death, resurrection, and the human soul's journey. Pay attention to the final movement, which features a soaring choral climax that conveys a sense of spiritual transcendence.

2. Ludwig van Beethoven Symphony No. 9 in D Minor, "Choral"
Listening Guide: Beethoven's Ninth Symphony is celebrated for its final movement, which includes the "Ode to Joy." It's a joyful and triumphant ode to the human spirit and unity. Listen for the transformation from darkness to light throughout the symphony.

3. Richard Strauss Also sprach Zarathustra
Listening Guide: This tone poem is inspired by Friedrich Nietzsche's philosophical work and explores themes of human existence

and evolution. The opening fanfare, famously used in the film "2001: A Space Odyssey," evokes a sense of cosmic exploration and awakening.

4. Ralph Vaughan Williams Symphony No. 5 in D Major
Listening Guide: Vaughan Williams' Fifth Symphony is often seen as a reflection on the human condition and the search for solace and transcendence. The serene third movement, with its lush string melodies, captures a sense of inner peace.

5. John Tavener "The Protecting Veil"
Listening Guide: This modern composition for cello and orchestra is inspired by Eastern Orthodox spirituality. It's contemplative and meditative, inviting the listener to reflect on the mystical and the divine.

6. Arvo Pärt "Tabula Rasa"
Listening Guide: Pärt's minimalist composition invites introspection and spiritual contemplation. "Fratres" and "Spiegel im Spiegel" are particularly notable for their simplicity and emotional depth.

7. Samuel Barber "Adagio for Strings"
Listening Guide: Barber's "Adagio for Strings" is renowned for its emotional intensity and has been described as a musical expression of human suffering and longing. It's often used in contexts related to mourning and reflection.

8. Olivier Messiaen "Quartet for the End of Time"
Listening Guide: Written during Messiaen's internment in a German prisoner-of-war camp during World War II, this quartet explores themes of faith, transcendence, and the apocalypse. Each movement has its own spiritual significance.

These orchestral compositions offer profound musical journeys that resonate with the themes of self-discovery, spirituality, and the human quest for meaning. Listening to these works with an open heart and mind can provide a deep and enriching experience.

My Choices

1. Yes "Relayer" (1974)

Listening Guide: "Relayer" was released in 1974 and is known for its complex and intricate musical compositions. The album features three tracks: "The Gates of Delirium," "Sound Chaser," and "To Be Over," each showcasing the band's virtuosity and progressive rock style.

Track 1: "The Gates of Delirium"

Duration: Approximately 21 minutes
Overview: "The Gates of Delirium" is an epic and ambitious track that features multiple sections and shifts in tempo and mood. It's inspired by Leo Tolstoy's novel "War and Peace" and explores themes of war and peace, conflict, and resolution. The track includes energetic instrumental passages, powerful vocals by Jon Anderson, and a sense of drama.
Listening Tips: Pay attention to the various musical themes and how they evolve throughout the song. The battle section in the middle is particularly intense and showcases the band's virtuosity.

Track 2: "Sound Chaser"

Duration: Approximately 9 minutes
Overview: "Sound Chaser" is a more compact and fast-paced track that features intricate instrumental interplay, particularly between guitarist Steve Howe and keyboardist Patrick Moraz. The lyrics are somewhat abstract and focus on the idea of chasing sound and rhythm.
Listening Tips: Enjoy the intricate and frenetic instrumental work, as well as the dynamic shifts in tempo and style.

Track 3: "To Be Over"

Duration: Approximately 9 minutes
Overview: "To Be Over" serves as a mellower and more melodic conclusion to the album. It features acoustic guitar, gentle vocals by Jon Anderson, and a sense of reflection. The lyrics express themes of renewal and transcendence.

Listening Tips: Take in the soothing and contemplative mood of this track, which contrasts with the complexity of the preceding songs.

Overall Listening Tips:

Open Ears: "Relayer" is a progressive rock masterpiece with intricate instrumental passages and complex compositions. Approach it with an open mind and ears to appreciate its depth.

Instrumental Interplay: Pay attention to the interplay between the various instruments, including guitar, keyboards, and percussion. Yes is known for its virtuosic musicianship.

Conceptual Themes: Consider the conceptual themes explored in the album, especially in "The Gates of Delirium."

Dynamic Range: "Relayer" has moments of high energy and intensity as well as moments of subtlety and reflection. Notice how the band navigates these dynamics.

"Relayer" is a challenging and rewarding album that showcases Yes's progressive rock prowess. It's a work that benefits from multiple listens to fully appreciate its complexity and depth.

"Soon" is the closing track on Yes' 1974 album "Relayer." It is the shortest song on the album and is known for its melodic and soothing qualities. "Soon" features Jon Anderson's distinctive vocals and lyrics that convey a sense of hope and optimism.

The song "Soon" is often regarded as one of Yes' more accessible and emotionally resonant compositions. It serves as a contrast to the complex and lengthy tracks that precede it on the album, particularly "The Gates of Delirium" and "Sound Chaser."

§

2. Yes "Tales from Topographic Oceans" (1973)
Jon Anderson, the lead vocalist of the progressive rock band Yes,

received a copy of "Autobiography of a Yogi" by Paramahansa Yogananda from Jamie Muir at Bill Bruford's wedding on 3 March 1973. Anderson's fascination with a particular footnote on page **83** of the book reportedly served as an inspiration for much of the material he wrote for the album "Tales from Topographic Oceans."

Listening Guide:
"Tales from Topographic Oceans" is the sixth studio album by the British progressive rock band Yes. It was released in 1973 and is one of the band's most ambitious and controversial works. Here's some information about the album:

1. Double Album: "Tales from Topographic Oceans" is a double album, consisting of four lengthy tracks, each taking up an entire side of the LP. The album's total duration is over 80 minutes.

2. Conceptual Work: The album is a conceptual work based on a series of lyrical and philosophical ideas developed by Jon Anderson, the band's lead vocalist. Each of the four tracks corresponds to one of these ideas or "tales."

3. Complex and Experimental: Musically, the album is characterized by its complexity, featuring intricate arrangements, time signature changes, and extensive instrumental passages. It's known for its progressive and experimental nature.

4. Controversy: "Tales from Topographic Oceans" received mixed reviews upon its release. Some fans and critics praised its ambition and musicality, while others found it overly indulgent and self-indulgent. It remains a divisive album in Yes' discography.

5. Commercial Success: Despite the mixed critical reception, the album performed well commercially. It reached the top of the UK Albums Chart and peaked at No. 6 on the Billboard 200 chart in the United States.

6. Legacy: Over the years, "Tales from Topographic Oceans" has gained a dedicated following, and it is still regarded as a significant work in the progressive rock genre. It's considered one of Yes' most adventurous and challenging albums.

The album's four tracks are:

"The Revealing Science of God (Dance of the Dawn)"
"The Remembering (High the Memory)"
"The Ancient (Giants Under the Sun)"
"Ritual (Nous sommes du soleil)"

Each of these tracks explores different musical themes and concepts, making "Tales from Topographic Oceans" a complex and immersive listening experience.movement, with its lush string melodies, captures a sense of inner peace.

"Tales from Topographic Oceans" is a complex and lengthy album, with each of its four tracks taking up an entire side of the LP. It's a work that rewards patient and attentive listening. Here's a listening guide to help you navigate the album:

Side One: "The Revealing Science of God (Dance of the Dawn)"

Duration: Approximately 22 minutes
Overview: The opening track is divided into several sections, each with its own musical themes and dynamics. It begins with a gentle, melodic introduction featuring acoustic guitar and Jon Anderson's vocals. As the piece progresses, it becomes more complex, with intricate instrumental passages and shifts in tempo. The lyrics explore themes of enlightenment and spiritual awakening.
Listening Tips: Pay attention to the evolving musical motifs and the interplay between different instruments. The track has moments of both tranquility and intensity.

Side Two: "The Remembering (High the Memory)"

Duration: Approximately 20 minutes
Overview: "The Remembering" is a reflective and introspective piece. It features lush arrangements, including synthesizers, acoustic guitar, and mellotron. The lyrics delve into themes of memory, past experiences, and the search for meaning.
Listening Tips: Allow yourself to immerse in the atmospheric and dreamlike quality of this track. The mellotron and synthesizer work is particularly noteworthy.

Side Three: "The Ancient (Giants Under the Sun)"

Duration: Approximately 19 minutes
Overview: "The Ancient" is a multi-part composition that explores different musical styles, from folk-inspired acoustic sections to more rock-oriented moments. The lyrics draw on mythological and ancient themes.
Listening Tips: Pay attention to the shifts in musical style and tempo. This track showcases the band's versatility and willingness to experiment with different sounds.

Side Four: "Ritual (Nous sommes du soleil)"

Duration: Approximately 21 minutes
Overview: "Ritual" is a dynamic and dramatic composition that features strong percussion, energetic guitar work, and intricate vocal harmonies. The lyrics touch on themes of ritual and celebration.
Listening Tips: This track has a sense of grandeur and theatricality. Listen for the powerful interplay between the musicians, especially the percussion and guitar sections.

Overall Listening Tips:

Patience: "Tales from Topographic Oceans" is a lengthy and intricate work. Take your time to absorb each track and appreciate its nuances.
Lyrics: Consider reading the lyrics as you listen, as they provide insights into the thematic content of each piece.
Instrumentation: Pay attention to the wide range of instruments used throughout the album, from synthesizers and mellotrons to acoustic and electric guitars.
Mood and Themes: Reflect on the mood and themes of each track and how they relate to the overall concept of the album.

Remember that "Tales from Topographic Oceans" is a progressive rock masterpiece known for its complexity and depth. It may take multiple listens to fully appreciate the intricacies of the music and lyrics.

§

3. "Sarangi: The Voice of a Hundred Colors" by Ustad Sultan Khan (1969)
A captivating album that showcases the virtuosity of this legendary sarangi maestro. This listening guide will help you appreciate the beauty and depth of the music on this album:

Album Overview:
Artist: Ustad Sultan Khan
Album: "Sarangi: The Voice of a Hundred Colors"
Genre: Indian Classical Music (Sarangi)
Duration: Varies by track

Track-by-Track Listening Guide:

1. Raga Ahir Bhairav (Alap, Jod, and Jhala):
Duration: Approximately 23 minutes
Overview: Begin your journey with the serene and meditative Raga Ahir Bhairav. This track features the slow and melodic Alap, followed by the rhythmic Jod and the energetic Jhala. Listen to the gradual development of the raga and the expressive nuances in Ustad Sultan Khan's sarangi playing.

2. Raga Madhuvanti:
Duration: Approximately 10 minutes
Overview: "Raga Madhuvanti" offers a change of pace with its sweet and melodious character. Pay attention to the intricate melodic patterns and the emotional depth conveyed by the sarangi.

3. Raga Kafi:
Duration: Approximately 13 minutes
Overview: In "Raga Kafi," experience the versatility of the sarangi as it navigates through the complexities of this raga. Note the sarangi's ability to evoke a myriad of emotions, from joy to introspection.

4. Raga Jaijaivanti:
Duration: Approximately 11 minutes
Overview: Conclude your listening experience with "Raga Jaijaivanti." Appreciate the sarangi's ability to convey the playful and joyful aspects of this raga. The interplay between the artist's skill and the raga's vibrant melodies is a highlight.

Listening Tips:
Find a quiet and peaceful environment to fully immerse yourself in the music.

Consider reading about the specific ragas featured on the album to gain a deeper understanding of their emotional and melodic characteristics.

Pay attention to the nuances in Ustad Sultan Khan's sarangi playing, including the use of slides (meends) and ornamentations (gamaks). Allow the music to evoke emotions and take you on a meditative journey through the rich tapestry of Indian classical music.

"Sarangi: The Voice of a Hundred Colors" is a testament to the mastery of Ustad Sultan Khan and the expressive capabilities of the sarangi. It offers a profound and soul-stirring listening experience, inviting you to explore the myriad shades of emotion conveyed through this enchanting instrument.

The Sarangi

I love the sound of the Sarangi. There is no instrument that transports and informs and cajoles and breaks your heart quite like this instrument. While it may not be as widely known as some other Indian instruments, its contribution to the classical and folk music traditions is significant and deserves to be known the world over.

The sarangi is a traditional Indian musical instrument with a rich history, distinct playing techniques, and a significant role in Indian music. Here's an overview of the sarangi:

History:
The sarangi's origins can be traced back to the Indian subcontinent, likely in the 18th century or earlier. It is believed to have evolved from earlier bowed instruments.

The word "sarangi" is derived from two Sanskrit words: "saar" (meaning "with") and "angee" (meaning "a sound"), emphasizing its role as an instrument that produces a rich and diverse range of sounds.

Playing Techniques:
The sarangi is played with a bow and consists of three or four main strings, along with numerous sympathetic strings beneath the main ones.

It is a challenging instrument to master due to its lack of frets and its reliance on precise finger placement and pressure to produce the desired pitches.

Sarangi players use their fingernails to press the strings against the fingerboard, allowing for microtonal nuances and ornamentations. The instrument is known for its ability to mimic the human voice, and skilled players can produce a wide range of tonal variations and expressive qualities.

Region of Origin:
The sarangi is particularly associated with North Indian classical music, including genres such as Hindustani classical music. It is commonly found in the northern regions of India, including Rajasthan, Uttar Pradesh, and Punjab, where it has been an integral part of traditional music for centuries.

Construction:
Sarangis are typically handcrafted from wood, often using materials like teak, mahogany, or tun wood for the body. The soundbox of the sarangi is often carved with intricate designs, adding to its aesthetic appeal. The strings are typically made from materials like gut or steel.

Importance to Indian Music:
The sarangi is considered one of the most expressive and soulful instruments in Indian music. Its ability to closely emulate vocal melodies makes it invaluable for classical vocal accompaniment. It is a popular instrument for solo and ensemble performances, often used in classical, semi-classical, and folk music traditions. The sarangi's role is not limited to Indian classical music; it has also been used in various regional folk and devotional music styles.

The sarangi is a deeply rooted and cherished instrument in Indian music. Its unique playing techniques, rich history, and ability to convey deep emotions have made it an indispensable part of the musical heritage of North India.

4. Paul Winter's "Icarus" (1972)

is a landmark album in the world of jazz and fusion music. The album was produced by George Martin, who is best known for his extensive work as the producer of The Beatles. George Martin's production on "Icarus" contributed to the album's unique fusion of musical styles and its innovative sound.

Album Overview:

Artist: Paul Winter Consort
Album: "Icarus"
Genre: Jazz, Fusion, World Music
Release Date: 1972

History:

"Icarus" was released by the Paul Winter Consort in 1972. Paul Winter is an American saxophonist and bandleader known for his pioneering work in world music and environmental activism.

The album is often considered a groundbreaking work that blends jazz improvisation with elements of classical music, world music, and environmental sounds.

It was inspired by the myth of Icarus, who flew too close to the sun, and the album's music is intended to evoke a sense of flight and exploration.

Track-by-Track Listening Guide:

1. Icarus:

Duration: Approximately 7 minutes
Overview: The album opens with the title track, "Icarus." It sets the tone for the entire album with soaring saxophone melodies, lush orchestration, and a sense of boundless freedom. The piece captures the essence of Icarus' mythical flight.

2. Icarus: Theme for Two Flutes:

Duration: Approximately 3 minutes
Overview: This short piece features two flutes dancing together in a playful and harmonious manner. It provides a delicate contrast to the more expansive compositions on the album.

3. Icarus: Interlude:
Duration: Approximately 1 minute
Overview: "Icarus: Interlude" is a brief, atmospheric segment that adds texture and ambiance to the album.

4. Icarus: Icarus 4:
Duration: Approximately 9 minutes
Overview: "Icarus 4" continues the musical journey with complex arrangements and saxophone improvisations. It explores various moods and textures, from serene to dramatic.

5. Icarus: Rural Space:
Duration: Approximately 5 minutes
Overview: "Rural Space" introduces a pastoral and contemplative atmosphere, featuring acoustic guitar and the sounds of nature. It provides a reflective pause in the album's narrative.

6. Icarus: Minotaur:
Duration: Approximately 7 minutes
Overview: "Minotaur" brings a sense of tension and intrigue to the album, with its dynamic shifts and rhythmic complexities. It represents the mythical labyrinth and the challenge of facing the Minotaur.

7. Icarus: Icarus 5:
Duration: Approximately 9 minutes
Overview: The album concludes with "Icarus 5," a powerful and expansive piece that revisits themes from earlier tracks. It soars to a majestic climax, capturing the essence of Icarus' fateful flight.

Listening Tips:
Approach "Icarus" as a cohesive musical journey that tells a story through its tracks.

Pay attention to Paul Winter's expressive saxophone playing and the ensemble's intricate arrangements.

Enjoy the blend of jazz, classical, and world music influences that create a unique fusion sound.

Let your imagination roam as you listen, connecting the music to the mythological tale of Icarus and his flight.

Provisions

In W. Somerset Maugham's novel "The Razor's Edge," Larry Darrell primarily visits the following places in India:

1. Bombay (Mumbai): Larry initially arrives in Bombay, which serves as the starting point of his journey in India. He spends some time in the city before moving on to other locations.

2. Rishikesh: Larry spends a significant part of his time in Rishikesh, a holy city in northern India along the Ganges River. It is in Rishikesh that he delves deeper into his spiritual quest and seeks guidance from spiritual teachers.

While Larry's journey in India is a significant aspect of the novel, specific details about the cities he visits and the experiences he has may vary in different adaptations and interpretations of the story. Therefore, it's important to refer to the original novel for the most accurate account of his travels in India.

In 1925, a person of limited income, like Larry Darrell from "The Razor's Edge," would have had access to affordable and simple food options in both Bombay (Mumbai) and Rishikesh. Here are some typical foods that he might have encountered in these locations:

Bombay (Mumbai):

1. Street Food: Mumbai is renowned for its street food culture. Larry might have enjoyed affordable and delicious street snacks like vada pav (a spicy potato fritter sandwich), pav bhaji (a spiced vegetable curry served with bread rolls), and bhel puri (a snack made from puffed rice, vegetables, and chutneys).

2. Pav: Pav, a type of bread roll, is a common accompaniment to many Mumbai dishes. It's inexpensive and often used in various street food items.

3. Dosa: South Indian dishes like dosa (thin rice crepes) and idli (steamed rice cakes) are popular and budget-friendly options in Mumbai. They are typically served with coconut chutney and sambar (a lentil-based vegetable stew).

4. Poha: Poha is a simple and affordable breakfast dish made from flattened rice, often seasoned with spices, mustard seeds, and curry leaves.

5. Chai: Larry might have enjoyed a cup of chai (Indian tea) from a roadside stall. Chai was and still is a popular and inexpensive beverage option in India.

Rishikesh:

1. Ashram Meals: Many ashrams in Rishikesh offer vegetarian meals to seekers and travelers. These meals are simple, nutritious, and reasonably priced. They typically consist of rice, dal (lentil soup), chapatis (flatbreads), and vegetables.

2. Local Vegetarian Restaurants: In Rishikesh, there are small vegetarian restaurants that serve budget-friendly thali meals. Thali is a platter that includes a variety of dishes, such as rice, dal, sabzi (vegetable curry), and chutneys.

3. Fruits and Fresh Produce: Rishikesh is located in a region with abundant fruit and vegetable markets. Larry might have bought fresh fruits and vegetables from local markets, which would have been economical and healthy options.

4. Simple Snacks: Snacks like pakoras (deep-fried fritters) and samosas are available at street stalls and local eateries and are often quite affordable.

During his time in Bombay and Rishikesh, Larry Darrell's limited income would have allowed him to experience the local cuisine without straining his budget. The emphasis in both places would likely have been on vegetarian meals due to dietary preferences and affordability.

Bombay (Mumbai), late 1920s

In the 1925-1930 era, Mumbai's street food culture was already vibrant. The city's bustling streets offered an array of budget-friendly delights like vada pav, pav bhaji, and bhel puri. These flavorful and affordable snacks showcased the rich tapestry of flavors that defined Mumbai's culinary heritage, captivating the taste buds of locals and visitors alike.

May Goddess Saraswati, who is fair like the jasmine-colored moon, and whose pure white garb is like the snow, and who is adorned with the veena and blessed with a lotus seat, reside on my head.
May Goddess Lakshmi, who is beautifully adorned and seated on a lotus, and who rids us of all troubles, reside in my speech.
And may Goddess Saraswati and Goddess Lakshmi bestow their blessings upon me.

§

This prayer is often recited to seek blessings from the divine for knowledge, wisdom, and prosperity, and it can be used as a farewell or goodbye prayer as well.

The prayer is often referred to as the "Saraswati Vandana" or "Saraswati Mantra," is a traditional Hindu prayer dedicated to Goddess Saraswati, the Hindu deity of knowledge, music, arts, wisdom, and learning. Goddess Saraswati is revered in Hinduism as the embodiment of all knowledge and the arts.

The exact origin of this prayer is not attributed to a specific author or time period. It is part of the rich tradition of devotional and philosophical poetry in Hinduism. Prayers and hymns dedicated to deities like Saraswati have been composed and passed down through generations orally and in written form.

This particular prayer is widely recited by students, scholars, and devotees of Goddess Saraswati to seek her blessings for knowledge, wisdom, and success in their academic and creative pursuits. It is a heartfelt expression of devotion to the goddess and has become an integral part of Hindu religious and cultural practices.

While the specific authorship and origin may not be known, it continues to be an important part of Hindu rituals, especially during Saraswati Puja and other occasions dedicated to the goddess.

www.ingramcontent.com/pod-product-compliance
Lightning Source LLC
Chambersburg PA
CBHW051626120626
46551CB00014B/1951